Just Show Up

Just Show Up

Steps You Can Take To Become the Courageous Leader You Were Meant to Be

Debi Grebenik, Ph.D.

Copyright © 2022 by
Debi Grebenik, Ph.D.

All rights reserved.
This book, or parts thereof, may not be
reproduced in any form without permission.

Distributed globally by Boss Media.
New York | Los Angeles | London | Sydney

Hardback ISBN: 978-1-63337-665-6
E-Book ISBN: 978-1-63337-666-3
LCCN: 2022917106

Printed in the United States of America
1 3 5 7 9 10 8 6 4 2

Dedication

Most people write dedications with flowery language about all the people to whom they are indebted. That reads as a great tribute and one that importantly highlights those who marked their journeys. For me, my dedication is to those in my life who told me it was time—time for me to invest in myself; time to write; time to risk and time to follow my heart. They didn't just tell me, they then encouraged me along the way when self-doubt began to creep in.

My group is small and mainly consisted of my husband of 44 years who is always cheering me on in my next adventure. We all need an encourager like he is—he celebrates me while also picking up any slack that he can so that I can do what I feel called to do.

My adult children, Dole, Tosh, and Kristen also encouraged me to pursue my dream, stating that it was about time. Their spouses, Lindsley, Ashlyn, and Pat also jumped in with their encouragement. And let me not forget my grandchildren who give me the courage to try hard things, to dream big, to not take myself too seriously, and to enjoy each and every moment as a fun adventure.

And finally, God's blessings run deep in my life and this book reminds me of how His plan brought all of these experiences together for me. For His calling in my life, and for those who believed in me, I am humbly grateful.

Contents

Introduction 1

Chapter 1: A Different Perspective on Leadership 3

Chapter 2: Shame, Blame, and the Trauma Train 29

Chapter 3: Why Are We Talking About Fear? 49

Chapter 4: Looking Out For the Pebble in Your Shoe 71

Chapter 5: Who is Walking With You? 85

Chapter 6: Building Your Power Walkers 103

Chapter 7: And Now What? 121

Chapter 8: Now You Become the Teacher 135

References 151

Introduction

Thank you for picking up this book. It was created in relationships—with those I supervise; those I followed and those I admired. My family taught me so much in this process. I learned from difficult feedback, mistakes, successes, laughter, joy and coaching. I read books, went to trainings, and analyzed myself, others, and anything I could in my efforts to learn from and understand what leadership is. This is a compilation of my learnings with the hope that you might be able to glean and learn something from my journey. I tried to be as transparent and vulnerable as I could, believing that there would be benefit in truth-telling. May God speak to you through these words—His words. Leadership is a relational process; we are leading humans, not projects. Never forget that.

This book intends to challenge you to look at leadership differently-focusing on how you show up, not what you know or do. Each chapter addresses a different dimension related to what steps you can take in your leadership journey that will advance your effectiveness. Practical steps, leadership concepts, combined with personal stories create the narratives of how you can show up. Be willing to be challenged and to question your long-held beliefs.

Just Show Up

Space is provided to reflect on questions provided throughout each chapter.

My hope for you is that God speaks to your heart as you enter into this space. As a result, I would love to hear from you- what you learned and what you would add to this content.

> "The courage to be vulnerable is not about winning or losing. It's about the courage to show up when you can't predict or control the outcome." Brené Brown

> "The willingness to show up changes us. It makes us a little braver each time." Brené Brown

> "…showing up means facing into your thoughts, emotions, and behaviors willingly, with curiosity and kindness." Susan David (Emotional Agility)

CHAPTER 1

A different perspective on leadership

Step into looking at leadership differently

I am not quite sure why you picked up this book; yet, I am glad you decided to join me on this journey. Let's explore our collective leadership journeys together. I wish we were in the same room, sharing a cup of hot coffee and chatting about where you are in your path. We would share a few laughs and some insights with each other. I hope that you'll reach out and share what you are learning. I imagine we would be friends, inspiring and challenging each other. Leadership is relationship-based, that is where the effective work occurs.

I thought that leadership involved knowing everything—I've lived my life in my academic pursuit, thinking that was the way. If only I were smart enough, I would be accepted. If I knew what to do, when to do it, and how to do it, then of course others would follow me, and I would be the leader I wanted to be. And others would see that I am a leader. The truth was that this formula wasn't the one that I needed. Stay tuned and hear about my journey and see if you see a little bit of yourself along the way. You might even relate to some of my missteps. Hopefully we can both find some wisdom as we talk about leadership. This isn't that book that spouts theories and hyperbole, rather, I get gritty and talk about what leadership looks like when it's lived out—with flaws, missteps, joy, and even some successes.

It makes sense that I thought being smart enough was the answer and the road to effective leadership. In my family, my identity was rooted in my intelligence and performance. I felt pressure to get the grades, to excel, and to perform. I was only doing what I'd always done. I took that same mentality into the workplace, believing that the magic formula was to be smart enough—yet I didn't know who would decide what "enough" was. What I learned in the process is that my intelligence was not enough, not even close. When I experienced my first leadership opportunities, no one talked to me about leadership. The closest I came to a mentor was looking up the definition in the dictionary. So, I was making it up as I went and not doing a very good job at it. You know the formula, you do your job well, get good feedback, start to feel confident, and then you are promoted to a supervisory position. We do well in one role so the assumption is if we are promoted we will do well in that role; however, the role of worker or doer is very different than leadership roles and requirements. And the road for preparation for leadership is often non-existent.

My way of learning is typically through books and when we are overwhelmed or in new territory, we gravitate toward the known or familiar and that is exactly where I went. As I devoured leadership books, they consistently talked about how to build teams, run meetings, manage finances, and other administrative tasks. I thought that because these topics were what the books addressed, these were the stepping stones that would transform me into an effective leader. It was a good start, and yet I still needed to learn a lot.

The funny thing is that when I followed the concepts presented in the books that I consulted, I didn't magically reach that goal of becoming an amazing and revered leader. In fact, the opposite happened; I was failing and couldn't figure out why. You could almost tell which book I was reading because those were the concepts I worked on that day, week or month. I didn't really know how to integrate the learning, I just practiced what the book said.

Unfortunately, my concept of leadership was skewed because I thought my role as the leader was to tell people what to do. My perception was that I needed to give answers, solve problems, create business, and balance budgets. You can imagine how well that was received. I missed so much about what leadership is really about.

This image of a leader that I developed in my head was truly a blind spot for me. I didn't really know anything different, and no one showed me the way. None of my supervisors up to this point in time demonstrated anything that I wanted to emulate. No one I knew was talking about leadership, so I didn't ask. I observed others and began to develop a comprehensive list of everything I *didn't* want to do.

During one of my first evaluations as a new supervisor, I received feedback that was very critical of my supervisory skills. I was shocked and my breath was taken away as I listened to very difficult feedback. The feedback was very deficit-based without highlighting any of my strengths or without providing me any direction on how I could move forward.

This was a turning point for me; I knew something needed to change. I wasn't quite sure what I needed to do or how I would do it; however, I knew that if I didn't figure something out, I would keep doing the same things and end up with the same results. And no one was helping me find my way—they just expected me to figure it out, and that's not a very effective supervisory strategy. I also felt as though I wasn't living according to my values. Something had to change or I probably would need to change careers.

Knowing that I spent a lot of time without living according to my values, I knew I needed to change something. I also knew the change needed to be pretty dramatic because I was stuck. Because of my litany of mistakes and my ineffective leadership style, I sought out those that I supervised during my less than stellar supervisory days. Apologizing for my ineptness and for the harm I caused, I showed up with humility as I owned my mistakes. Graciously I was forgiven, and my hope was that even though I would make many more mistakes, I didn't want to repeat the same ones. I wanted to leave behind the days of telling others what to do and how to do it. I was motivated and ready—still without answers, yet I felt that I could learn. Isn't this where God wants us to be? When we come to Him, knowing that we lack wisdom, we can ask God who gives generously to all without finding fault and it will be given to him. (James 1:5). The Webster's Unabridged Dictionary defines wisdom as "knowledge, and the capacity to make due use of it." Isn't that a good working definition? I already built a good knowledge base, now I needed God to give me the wisdom to know how to use that knowledge. I was getting excited about the journey ahead. I don't think God requires us to know all the answers; my assessment is that He wants us to be teachable. When we show up as teachable, He will pour into us.

Step into self-compassion

As part of moving forward, I needed to forgive myself; that was probably the most difficult part of this journey. I needed to move on and release my shame for how much I messed up those early leadership attempts. My heart and desires were to be an effective leader, and the reality is that I fell short of the mark. I worked hard so that when I failed, my hope was that I would fall forward and learn from my experiences. So, there is where my story starts—with my failure and the lessons learned and changes made because of those failures. If we listen, our mistakes and failures will speak to us. All we need is to be sure that we show up as teachable as previously mentioned. Now let's look at what some of those failures taught me. It is a journey and may include some detours, speed bumps, U-turns and maybe even exploring some new destinations.

 While I adjusted and tried to improve, I still needed to learn so much. Again, I was entering into roles that I was ill-prepared for. I became a director of a residential treatment center, and suddenly everyone was looking to me for answers. I made up a lot of answers so I wouldn't disappoint my staff who were looking to me. This period marks another big growth spurt. I was focused too much on providing solutions rather than on learning how to lead, so once again I found myself in that loop of relying on my intellect to solve problems. Instead, I needed to be listening, which would help me build relationships, motivate others, and create vision. It's even important to listen to what isn't said—now that takes practice. This means paying attention to body language, tone of voice, nuance, and intensity of responses.

Without answers, I was floundering. I was trying to please both those I supervised and those that supervised me. I changed directions and still didn't yield the results I yearned for. Seriously, how did others lead and do it so effortlessly? What I didn't realize is that others weren't leading effortlessly, it just looked that way. The more I reached out, the more I learned I wasn't alone in my journey. I felt as though I were wandering in the wilderness, without the luxury of God's daily provision of manna. I was just becoming aware of what I didn't know, and this lack of knowledge caused my insecurities to manifest. Leading from a place of internal weakness is certainly not the leadership vision I imagined for myself.

I thought that a graduate degree would induct me into the "land of the knowing." My degrees got me in the game; I just didn't own the playbook. I didn't know what to do, how to do it, or when to do it. This is such a recurring theme that you are probably tiring of hearing it. In response to this reality, I began my discovery process. It was difficult to step into the unknown, yet gradually the unknown became the known. Part of my learning process came from messing things up, understanding my mistakes, and then moving on. The failures were embarrassing at times because I wanted others to think that I knew what I was doing: I liked appearing competent and knowledgeable—who doesn't?

Debi Grebenik, Ph.D.

Step into learning

One of my big lessons came from a supervisor I will call John (obviously not his real name). Some days I could do no wrong; other days I could do nothing right. I was caught in the cycle of trying to do what I thought he wanted rather than working from my values or from what I knew to be true. I was working hard to appease those who were my supervisors because I needed my job. I truly lost my way, leading from a place of fear and survival. It is hard to lead others when you are engaged in your own internal conflict of working from a place that is contrary to your values. Over a long period of time, this creates dissatisfaction with your job, yourself, and even with others. This process creat3es moral injury—you can lose your sense of self and purpose.

 I knew I couldn't keep this up. I was seriously thinking about my options: stay and be miserable, leave in my discontent, or to try to change and grow. I wish I could say that I chose the latter, and yet I didn't. I guess I wasn't ready yet. My supervisor's inconsistencies, combined with my own insecurities, made it difficult for me to stay. It seemed as if I were only reacting while I put fires out. I was on call twenty-four hours a day, seven days a week and was overwhelmed and approaching burn-out. I stayed three-and-a-half years in a position where crises were normal without validation or encouragement. I didn't feel seen or supported—two things I would soon learn were paramount to effective leadership. I was frustrated because it seemed that I was constantly in a reactionary mode, just surviving. I couldn't afford the price this job was costing me. So, not seeing any other viable options, I left. Something I learned after this experience is that to feel psychologically safe, we need to ***feel seen, heard, and valued.*** I didn't experience any of that and as a result, I felt that there weren't options for me other than leaving. Sadly, it is much easier to leave than to stay and work through any issues.

It took me about a year after leaving to detox all the negativity from the experience. I stayed hypervigilant to anything that might be perceived as criticism. I was the walking wounded; not healed. I also began to realize how important my work environment was to my wellbeing. I vowed that I would never get myself in this type of situation again and that commitment didn't waiver in my career and led me to choose my next positions very carefully. As my leadership journey continued, I would draw on many of the lessons learned from this job.

I took another less stressful job with lesser status and fewer opportunities for growth. It was safe and didn't require too much from me. I needed to take some time to regroup, find my way again, and heal. This part of my journey took me most of the next year. I didn't realize how much toxic stress was being housed in my mind and body and how much anxiety I was experiencing. I was also hypersensitive because of my former supervisor's criticism of me and my sense of not being able to please him no matter what I did. My idea, encouraged by my trusted circle of friends and family, was to find and build a position where I could be true to myself once again. Gratefully, I listened to the wise counsel of my trusted friends who showed up with my best wellbeing at the forefront of all they suggested. I appreciated and honored their input. This is an important resilience skill—find those who will coach and support you as you create your pathways and try out new options.

You see, I thought that I needed to learn a leadership lesson when what I really needed was a spiritual lesson. The world tells us that if we will just follow a certain formula, we will be a better leader, lose weight, be healthier, or become wealthy. That's why you will find a plethora of self-help books; we tend to be looking for quick answers or easy steps: however, there wasn't a formula that would magically transform me into the leader I wanted to be, the leader I thought I should be, or even the leader others wanted me to be. I needed to go through all this turmoil to prepare for the change that needed to occur within me. Various things were starting to come together.

One of the contributing factors to my growth was found through my work on my Ph.D. in Educational Leadership and Innovation. It was no small coincidence that my academic pursuits were focused on leadership and that my heart's desire was to be a leader that would honor God. My academic pursuits put me on a path of looking at different leadership styles—transactional, transformative, influential, and others. Max DePree grabbed my attention in his book, *Leadership is an art*, where he spoke about leading by serving. This concept resonated with me and began to change my mindset. Things were beginning to shift and they need to. While the answer wasn't an academic one, my academic pursuits shaped the choices I was making.

I remember one day when I was working at a boys' residential treatment center and helping to cook lunch for the young men who lived there. As I was cleaning the kitchen afterwards, one of the residents looked at me and said, "Mrs. G, why you doing the dishes? You the big boss." I looked at him and explained that I didn't want to ever ask anyone to do something I wasn't willing to do. He looked at me with skepticism yet seemed to accept this response. As I spoke those words, I heard them myself—that I need to serve to lead.

As my mindset shifted, my behaviors changed. A passage in Ephesians reads:

> ...and walk continually in love [that is, value one another—practice empathy and compassion, unselfishly seeking the best for others], just as Christ also loved you and gave himself up for us... (Ephesians 5:2 Amplified).

I thought leadership was just about what *I* knew and did, when the focus needed to be on the followers. Servant leadership puts others' needs at the forefront of what you are doing. How could I lead if no one were following? I needed to tend to those I was supervising and prioritize their needs. In serving them, I was leading them. This was not what I expected in leadership growth.

The pieces were starting to come together, and I was beginning to take steps in the right direction. When we look at the word *step* as a verb, it means to lift and set down one foot after the other, to walk somewhere or to move to a new position. According to Merriam Webster's dictionary, it also means to be on one's way (https://www.merriam-webster.com/dictionary/step). I really like the concept of steps, those are manageable and something we can quantify. Many of us where devices that count our steps daily to reach certain goals. So why not use steps to build our leadership journey?

I wanted to find my way and become a leader who builds others up. I was ready to take the steps to be on my way.

Therefore, see that you walk carefully [living life with honor, purpose, and courage; shunning those who tolerate and enable evil], not as the unwise, but as wise [sensible, intelligent, discerning people] (Ephesians 5:15 AMP).

Now the steps I needed to take were starting to make sense. I was beginning to know where I wanted to walk and I was ready to start. I hope you will want to join me. I encourage you to begin a journal or log to track your process. Sometimes we forget all that we encounter, learn, and create as we are moving forward.

Start here—what goals are you setting for your leadership journey?

_____

_____

_____

_____

Step into what others are saying about leadership

While good leaders are trailblazers and they make a path for others to follow. Great leaders; however, inspire their people to reach higher, dream bigger, and achieve greater. (https://www.forbes.com/sites/ilyapozin/2014/04/10/16-leadership-quotes-to-inspire-you-to-greatness/#39b67acd67ad)

Just Show Up

One important skill you can bring to your leadership team is inspiring them so they inspire their teams. Encourage them to dream big.

> "If your actions inspire others to dream more, learn more, do more and become more, you are a leader."
>
> —John Quincy Adams

> "Leadership is the capacity to translate vision into reality."
>
> —Warren Bennis

Teach and Learn

Be teachable and continue learning. Smart leaders know what they don't know. Lean in and learn. You can learn from the most unlikely places. Embrace all of the opportunities available and the lessons they provide.

Be Bold

Leadership involves taking risks. Jump in, being risk averse won't serve you well if you want to grow and lead. Your boldness will give your teams courage and will encourage them to take appropriate risks also.

> "I cannot give you the formula for success, but I can give you the formula for failure, which is: Try to please everybody."
>
> —Herbert Swope

Be Humble

Humility is the flipside of learning. As you learn, you can lean into your humility that you don't know everything. After all, you can't learn if you aren't humble about where you are and what you are working on.

> "No man will make a great leader who wants to do it all himself, or to get all the credit for doing it."
>
> —Andrew Carnegie

> "Outstanding leaders go out of their way to boost the self-esteem of their personnel. If people believe in themselves, it's amazing what they can accomplish."
>
> —Sam Walton

> "The challenge of leadership is to be strong, but not rude; be kind, but not weak; be bold, but not bully; be thoughtful, but not lazy; be humble, but not timid; be proud, but not arrogant; have humor, but without folly."
>
> —Jim Rohn

> "Successful leaders see the opportunities in every difficulty rather than the difficulty in every opportunity."
>
> —Reed Markha

Just Show Up

Step into taking steps

Walking requires deliberate steps, moving our feet one at a time. Sometimes we know our destination, and sometimes we just wander. I wanted to walk with my destination in mind. And I knew that I could certainly walk the path by myself because I am not afraid of being alone. Yet walking with someone adds so much to the journey. People in my everyday life weren't always available, so I began my walk with authors, experts, and those with experience. I looked to those I admired and those who could teach me. I read about successes, failures, theories, and strategies, and I was still questioning what to do with all this information. How could I find my way? Where and how should I start? I didn't want to mess this up; I wasn't afraid of failure yet felt as though I'd failed so much already that I wanted to find some successes. Was that arrogant of me? I don't know—I just was ready to get something right. YBH kept going through my mind…yes, but how?

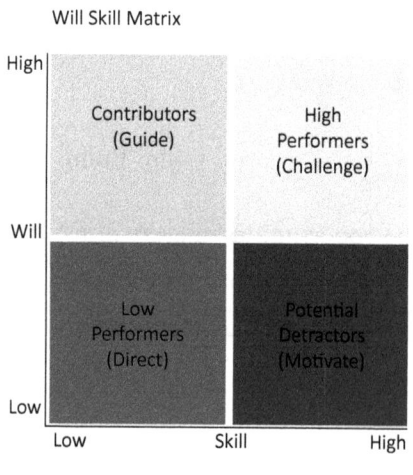

In my studies I saw a matrix with will and skills on the axes. I knew that I wanted to be in the quadrant of high performers that signified high skill and high will when in reality I was more in the contributors' quadrant. I was motivated and brought some experience to the process. https://www.stratechi.

com/will-skill-matrix/

All my steps were leading me in the same direction as I was beginning to find my way. The first step was simple, yet not easy. That first step set the pace, the direction, and the path for the steps that follow. Steps are incremental.

Let's look at our first step as foundational knowing it is based on the fact that it is not what you know, it's how you show up. What does that even mean? While it is helpful to understand leadership concepts and theories, because we are humans leading other humans, the person you *are* matters most. In the Old Testament, I am encouraged by David and how he shows up. He is a king with many flaws, yet God calls him a man after his own heart due to his zeal and passion for Him. While David made many mistakes (such as sleeping with another man's wife and then orchestrating the death of her husband), he was loved by God. I Chronicles 18:14 says "David reigned over all Israel, doing what was just and right for all his people." This is how he showed up—with compassion and concern for those he was leading. We remember how others make us feel—whether that is being built up or unappreciated.

How we show up includes our tone of voice, our energy, and our ability to be present. How we show up communicates that our work matters, that others matter, and even that I matter. How we show up creates the template and the footprint for the next steps.

Here are 5 ways you can show up:

1. Be fully present, not distracted or trying to do multiple things at one time such as checking your phone while someone is trying to talk to you. Communicate another's

value by giving them your whole-hearted attention. One time my son, who was eight years old at the time, was telling me something while I was cooking dinner. I thought I was doing a good job of listening and cooking at the same time. He quickly said he wanted me to listen, and I told him I was. He responded with "No, mom, listen with your eyes." He was telling me to be present in the moment. We can learn from this simple example—others know when we aren't fully present. Our presence is a special gift we give to others. With increased virtual and remote meetings, we need to try even harder to show our presence and engagement. Look for creative ways to demonstrate your attention.

2. Create calm and bring it to all that you are doing. Others will lean in and learn to trust your calm demeanor. Your calm will become their calm, and we can all experience more fun as the stress ebbs away. This is an important characteristic and one that I pray for and trust God to create in my life. I know at particularly difficult times, my staff would gravitate toward my office, stating that they just wanted to lean into my calm. I believe that we can catch calm from others.

3. Build fun into your work. This is probably one of my favorite ways of showing up. I like to play and laugh which builds our creativity. I remember one day when a business associate stopped by my office to get my signature on a contract. I told him that I only signed contracts after hula hooping. He skeptically looked at me, took off his sports jacket, and joined me in a one-minute hula hoop adventure. We laughed, I signed the contract, and the next year

our contract doubled. I can't say for sure that it was due to the hula hooping, yet hula-hooping sure didn't hamper our business negotiations. Additionally, after long or difficult leadership team meetings, we would hula hoop as a way to release and reset, to create levity and laughter.

4. Listen intentionally. Listen to hear what is said and what isn't said. Sometimes we need to pay more attention to body language, tone, and intensity than we do to words. This takes practice, yet the payoffs are significant. We can learn by listening to others' nonverbal cues or the emphasis given to their spaces.

5. Be aware of your own stuff. You know what I mean—your anxiety, sense of shame, fear, or frustration. You may think you are managing it, yet those unprocessed emotions can seep out through your body language, words, and even your tone. Self-awareness is imperative in the leadership process. Take the time to develop yours and then address your own emotional needs so that you can show up in a way that honors God, your values, and the leader you want to be. Don't be afraid to seek out therapeutic help if you think that will be beneficial. Do all you can to create your own healing.

I would be remiss if I didn't talk about the impact of trust in leadership. Without trust, we don't feel safe, and when we don't feel safe, we can't trust. Without trust or safety, we can't follow. Followers may find themselves in freeze, fight, or flight modes based on the situation and their past experiences. Here is how this plays out. A leader shares a suggested protocol with you about paid time off, stating that they want input on policy decisions. The next thing you know you receive an email discussing a new policy about paid time off that is distributed to all your staff. You don't recall being asked about the policy prior to its implementation. Several steps were missed in this process of implementation. Asking for feedback requires waiting to receive the requested input.

Collaboration grows at the speed of trust. As we grow our trust, our ability to collaborate and work with others grows. Building collaboration is an effective leadership skill.

When we can't depend on our leaders because our trust is compromised, the result is a perceived lack of safety. People tend to not leave jobs, they leave supervisors—and this might be one of the major reasons why. Trust and safety are the building blocks of an effective work environment. We can't move to growth or effective leadership when the foundation of trust is not built.

How you show up can create trust and safety. How do you want to manage those you work with or supervise? Only when people are confident that they are safe can they create, grow, and thrive. Safety and trust are grown in atmospheres of consistency, therefore messaging, expectations, and evaluation standards must be unchanging. When things are predictable and consistent, we trust them. This is why we drive the same way to work on a daily basis—it is known and we trust that path to work.

Clarity is an essential building block for both safety and trust. If my role and job expectations are unclear, I will be confused and unable to feel confident or competent. Brené Brown, professor and researcher from the University of Texas, says "clear is kind and unclear is unkind". That makes so much sense to me.

Even when you think you've been clear, you may need to repeat something to ensure clarity or ask if you are understood. This is a foundational building block in relationship-building, both personally and professionally, so be sure you don't skip or miss this step in your walk. If you try to build your team without taking the time to create safety and trust, you will need to circle back until you complete this step. Without trust, we can't move on to the next steps.

Let's take time to think about how you are going to get your steps in:

1. Pause to reflect on how you show up. This is the place to start. Work on your self-awareness. Ask for feedback. Observe how others respond to you. II Peter 1:6-7 tells us "…make every effort to add to your faith goodness; and to goodness, knowledge; and to knowledge, self-control; and to self-control, perseverance, and to perseverance; godliness, brotherly kindness, and to brotherly kindness, love. For if you possess these qualities in increasing measure, they will keep you from being ineffective and unproductive in your knowledge of our Lord Jesus Christ." Look at the order of this—self-control is very early on in the process, right after knowledge. So we are to know better and then do better so that we become better—know, do and be.

2. Ask others how they perceive you and be open to their feedback without being defensive. Ask those that you trust to give you input because not all of the feedback you get will be accurate or require change on your part.

3. Create a vision board for the type of leader you aspire to be. Include those who inspire and motivate you. Use this to visualize who you want to be and how you want to show up. Ask God to refine your vision, and He will speak to you as you trust Him to reveal His plan for you. You can include a life verse, a word, or even a picture that God gave you previously. Then put the board in a place where it will guide and remind you of God's plan for your leadership journey.

4. Identify what you want to avoid (inconsistencies, mixed messages, confusion). Sometimes it is easier to acknowledge what we don't want as opposed to what we want. Even identify words to avoid. Romans 12:17 tells us to "Be careful to do what is right in the eyes of everybody."

5. Identify what causes you to feel stressed. Include calming strategies you can use to regulate and manage your stress, and build a toolbox of what you can use to de-stress. Not only is this important for your own wellbeing, you are modeling this priority for those you are leading.

6. Create your own development plan that may include talking to someone, journaling, praying for wisdom, reading books, listening to podcasts, or anything else that helps you to learn and grow. Taking time to journal, pray, and reflect are also useful strategies. Seek understanding from God's word to lead you.

7. Find other leaders that you can talk to, question, and be challenged by, knowing that you can do the same for them. Create a safe group to process your leadership journey and to support

one another. Join women's leadership groups where you can discuss and challenge each other in a positive and safe group.

8. Choose your steps carefully. Start at the beginning, knowing that you may only be able to take a baby step. Remember that baby steps add up as we move forward. It's the small hacks in life that create the big changes. We don't lose twenty pounds at a time, we lose one pound, then two, and then three, leading us to our goal. Remember, just start…

9. Work on being authentic. Bring your whole self to your work and leadership, and pay attention to the areas where it is difficult to do so. Those might be places to work on. Authenticity is built on vulnerability and self-awareness.

10. Embrace and understand vulnerability. Don't hide your imperfections; let God use them for His glory. Let your flaws lead you, not defeat you. In our weaknesses will His strength be made perfect. This is also part of self-awareness. We don't need to focus on our flaws, we need to recognize them for what they are so they don't derail us from the journey God called us to.

Remember, God is not looking for perfection, so we shouldn't either. Does perfection even exist? The answer is a very strong *no*. Perfection is an illusion meant to leave us feeling defeated and worthless if we compare ourselves to others. God only asks that we give Him our best. Take this moment and ask God to fill you with His strength, His wisdom, and His power as preparation to take your first step. Write your prayer here and date it. Then wait and watch as God shows up in a mighty way.

Just Show Up

Now take a moment and think about ways to let go of perfectionism. This was also a difficult lesson for me to learn—and one that I am still learning. I got caught up in thinking that perfectionism demonstrated competence, so it was a worthy goal. Yet even when you realize that the whole concept is unachievable, it is still so hard to release it.

Is there an area of perfectionism you need to release? Write it here. Something in your personal or work lives?

_____

_____

_____

_____

As I began to grow in my understanding of the type of leader I wanted to be, I realized that I could no longer pursue perfectionism. Yet what was the alternative? Could I be okay with not knowing? With mistakes? With failure? These steps might be harder than I thought. I am okay with making mistakes and am comfortable with sharing my mistakes with others; however, I am afraid of others seeing me as incompetent. I was still trying to reconcile what I thought leadership was and what I was discovering it to be. I moved from thinking I could study, read, learn, and then perform to beginning to celebrate my imperfections. This was a significant shift for me, and I felt as though I were experiencing whiplash from this complete change of direction.

Could I make this change? Not only could I, I also wanted to engage with this change. I began trying out this new perspective with those I supervised as well as the leadership team I led. What I realized is that we want to follow someone we can relate to; not someone we perceive to be perfect. As I opened up, other leaders did as well. Be aware that vulnerability doesn't mean oversharing; it means being open about your feelings, experiences, and fears. I didn't need to share details, I could just share when I was struggling, concerned, or even confused. As I realized the value of being vulnerable, it became more important that I focused on ***how I showed up*** and on cultivating relationships. That became my mantra.

I wish I could say that I arrived; that I unlocked the key to becoming the leader I wanted to be; however, I started the journey and was excited for the next leg to begin. We can't become frozen in our analysis of how to perform, sometimes we just need to start. This requires embracing the uncertainties, the unknown, and even the messy parts of leadership and the insight, awareness, and growth required of leaders.

When we need to create change, one of the first steps is to envision where you want to go. Start with the end in mind. We seem to all know this. What we don't pay attention to is the transition period. It seems that we gear up for change as an event and don't prepare for the time it takes to implement the change. Change is behavioral; transition is the psychological component. Transition can be the time between the initiation of the change and the result. This time can be a neutral zone; a time when you are still partly in the old way and stepping into the new way. Think of Moses. He set out for the Promised Land and spent forty years wandering the wilderness or what we could consider the neutral zone. Can't you imagine those that joined him asking him "When will we ever get there? Do you know what you are doing? Why did we come this way? I thought we were going to the Promised Land. Why are we following you?" And Moses stayed God's course, even when it didn't make sense, when questions weren't answered and confusion was rampant. There are lessons to learn from Moses' steadfastness, even when questioned and misunderstood.

Leaders need to manage the transitions and in-between times. Ways to lead during times of uncertainty include clarity of the vision of where you are going. Consistent and clear communication is also key. Consistent and clear communication is also key. No, *that's not a typo*; that's a repeat of an important message. Another important component is to create consistency and predictability. When we create consistency and predictability, we build safety and trust. Your team will follow you when they feel safe and know they can trust you. And we're back to the same concept—it's not what you know; it's how you show up that makes you an effective leader. Leading through change and transition requires our attention to the anxiety, fears, and confusion that comes with change. It also requires attending to the people who are experiencing the change process and their anxiety, fears, and confusion. Leadership is one of the most unselfish roles you can ever participate in. Be prepared, you will be stretched more than you ever imagine.

Change is difficult because we want to protect the way things are and we want to avoid the unknown; and we want to stay where we are comfortable. Effective leaders tune into these needs; acknowledge and validate them and then work to meet them. I remember when I was focused on diversifying and growing the organization I was leading. I was excited about opportunity, innovation, and improved outcomes. I went after new contracts. I thrive on novelty and a fast pace. What I didn't consider was that not everyone was as keen about change as I was. Not only were they less than thrilled about all the new changes, but they were also not excited about the pace of change. You see, I missed bringing them along. I sped forward and then looked back and noticed they weren't following; I forgot an important principle. You need to bring people along at the pace they can manage and tolerate. While we didn't take on all the opportunities, I invited the team to work with me and choose what seemed to be the most viable. I pushed them to think strategically and to expand their comfort zone and they encouraged me to slow the pace down and to choose only those options that would be the most beneficial for the agency at that period. It was a great compromise. And our growth was measured, productive and sustainable. One caution to consider is that I tend to want to explain, defend and preserve my perspective so this was significant movement and growth for me. If you find yourself wanting to convince others of your perspective, that is a defensive modality—one that you should seek to avoid.

And yet another lesson for me to learn. I just never thought that leading would be so complicated. I thought that I could just work hard, study hard, and lead well. Now I am learning that I need to pay attention to my affect, my attitude, and my approach. I think this is what James meant in James 1:19 where he says to be quick to hear, slow to speak, and slow to anger. And I consistently pray for wisdom because God says when we lack wisdom, we can ask for it and God will give it generously without rebuke or blame. (James 1:5). By God's beautiful grace, we don't need to be worthy or earn the right to ask for wisdom. We can just ask. I like that. There is a small note that I keep on my desk, it says "Listen more, speak less, and don't freak out." Isn't that a good reminder? Sometimes we try all the things when what we need to do is to be still, observe, and ask God for wisdom and direction. Oh, if we could all do that?

CHAPTER 2

Shame, Blame, and the Trauma Train

Step into awareness

I would be remiss if I didn't take a moment to talk about trauma's impact on leadership. Many of us never stop to think about this. Trauma comes in multiple forms yet generally falls into two categories: developmental trauma which includes abuse and neglect or exposure to domestic violence, poverty, and racism; or event trauma such as a natural disaster, rape, car accidents, or other life-altering events. While trauma may seem psychological, the reality is that it shows up physiologically because we store the residue of its impact in our bodies. Let's explore how this plays out.

If you are a woman who experienced sexual abuse from a male relative (incest), you may not trust very easily, or you may feel anxiety around men. These are normal responses to abnormal occurrences. Maybe you were abandoned as a child, entered the foster care system and subsequently were adopted; you might find it difficult to trust people, or your anxiety levels might be significant. Perhaps you were exposed to domestic or community violence which resulted in a sense of hypervigilance and reactivity. Trauma is experiences as though it is occurring in a present tense reality. We may rationally believe that we shouldn't be bothered by our trauma because it happened years ago; yet, unless we engage in work that creates healing, the residue of trauma may still be evident and will sneak up on us. This is another reason why self-awareness is so vital to leaders.

Earlier we talked about effective leadership begins with how we show up. Now consider how those early experiences shape your worldview of people. You might find yourself slow to trust, very sensitive, and uncomfortable with change. Additionally, you might lack confidence or become stressed easily. We are typically very critical of ourselves and others who don't act in ways we think they should. What if we took a moment, gave grace, and realized that others' responses might be due to their personal trauma histories? Could that potentially redirect our shame and blame? Our trauma histories may cause behavioral or emotional responses that are unexpected and misunderstood.

Step into body awareness

Because trauma is stored in the body, it creates connections in our brains. If in our past, loud noises signaled that safety was compromised in their home; the message was perceived that someone was about to get hurt. Then, when we experience a loud voice or noise in present tense, we might find ourselves overreacting without knowing why. It can be very difficult to connect the dots between our past with our current behavior. Others may just see our reactions and assign intentionality to the behaviors, showing up with some element of judgment without meaning to. Then we feel judged, we can react to that sense of judgment, creating a cycle of blaming, hurt, and reactionary emotional responses. This can happen without our being aware of the process—we may only see the fallout that occurs from the cycle.

Let me give you an example. I trained on vicarious trauma for a large group of first responders, and afterwards one of the leaders (I'll call her "Marty") approached me and said that the training helped her understand how her own trauma history was affecting her ability to lead—her self-awareness was the beginning of her road to healing. And she was brave, vulnerable, and uncomfortable as she reached this realization. This is her story.

Marty was a very high-level successful leader; however, she realized that something was holding her back and that she wasn't realizing her potential. She wanted to know if I would meet with her individually. I agreed and we set aside an entire Saturday morning. When we met, I asked her to tell me her story (I kept it open open-ended so that she could start with whatever her pain points were). As she spoke, I noticed that her shoulder would pop up whenever she mentioned her mother. I shared my observation with her, and she said that there was no way that was happening. As she continued, I gently made this observation to her again. Marty then said, "Oh, okay; then maybe I need to try and figure out what that is about." This was a turning point for her awareness and healing. Then Marty began to tell me her *real* story.

When Marty's mom was pregnant, she contracted a disease that couldn't be treated while she was pregnant. Then after Marty was born, her mom opted to not get treatment because she was breastfeeding. When Marty was two, her mom passed away. Feeling the weight of her mother's life and death on her, Marty would shrug her shoulders when she spoke about her mom. This was her body's way of telling her it was too much to hold and that her body needed to shrug it off. Once I pointed this out to her, she let out a deep breath and said that she'd struggled with feelings of unworthiness for her entire life because her mother literally gave her entire life for her. This sense of being unworthy brought about shame and a relentless drive toward perfection. She became an overachiever focused on performance.

Her exhale was deep as I shared my observations with her and held the space for her to build her awareness. This allowed her to subsequently share her thoughts and feelings and make sense of them. Her realizations created a healing in her spirit so that she could show up in her personal and professional life differently. She began to realize that she was enough and worthy without achieving perfection. Can you imagine the relief that she felt in being able to let go of what she thought she needed to do or achieve to create the worthiness that would be worth her mother's life? Her relief was very visceral and evident in her countenance as well as her body's posture. A few tears were released as she began to let go and step into her new identity. Remember, this was only one conversation, where I reflected to her what I observed. I was still, observant, and brave enough to share my insights to her. I came to our time together—whether it is as a coach, clinician, or supervisor—prepared. I made sure I wasn't distracted. I prioritized being fully present so that I could be there for her in her own self-discovery. I like to think that I served as a barrier buster.

My role was not to be a fixer; rather, I gave her a safe space and time to process through her past and make sense of its current impact on her. This is also an example of listening to what wasn't said rather than focusing only on her words. Her body spoke truth, and with truth came freedom. Growth comes from freedom and creates effective leadership. Be sure you are listening to your own body as well as what others are telling you with theirs. This skill can become your superpower. Ask God for wisdom to see and hear what our bodies say.

A side effect of trauma is shame. We will talk about the visceral impact of shame throughout this chapter. Realize that shame may look uniquely different for each of us; we need to become aware of our own shame stories. Shame can shut us down or we can look to it for the lessons it will teach us. Shame, fear, and pain are difficult teachers, yet their lessons are significant. I want to learn from shame without living in it or staying stuck in it if at all possible. Most of us want to avoid pain if we can. I invite those in that give me empathy because that helps me to let go of the shame I am experiencing. I am so grateful that I don't live in the miry pits of shame; God's grace helped me to see my way out through forgiving myself and growing my awareness about how to stay out of that quagmire.

Step into discharging

Our bodies hold our pains, histories, trauma, joys, and our fears, and it may be demonstrated through psychosomatic reactions. Think of it this way; we need to listen to the messages our bodies are trying to communicate to us, without words and perhaps through metaphors. Sometimes our headaches are telling us that there's something we just can't get our head around. When you are experiencing a stomachache, that may be due to something that you just can't stomach. Sometimes our jaws ache, should we be asking ourselves if there is something we should be saying that we're afraid or reluctant to speak about? Our body knows best and tells us what it needs and what is wrong—we just aren't listening, or we listen too literally and don't look at the metaphorical messages. Sometimes we just need to step back and listen; create pauses in your life so that you can hear what your body is trying to tell you.

The book of Proverbs consistently states the connection between the mind and body. For example, Proverbs 17:22 says "A cheerful heart is good medicine, but a crushed spirit dries up the bones." Additionally, Hebrews 12:15 says "If you have a bitter root, it affects others whether you see it or not. By removing that bitter root, you preserve peace and faith among your relatives, friends, coworkers, and others. It's worth the fight not only for you but for everyone else who is involved." This connection not only impacts us personally, it can also spill over onto others-in positive and not so positive ways. I imagine this is no surprise to you and that you maybe you experienced the roll off of others' emotional content firsthand.

The mind-body connection began early as evidenced in Scripture:

> For you formed my inward parts; you knitted me together in my mother's womb. I praise you, for I am fearfully and wonderfully made. Wonderful are your works; my soul knows it very well. My frame was not hidden from you, when I was being made in secret, intricately woven in the depts of the earth. Your eyes saw my unformed substance; in your book were written, everyone one of them, the days that were formed for me, when yet there was none of them (Psalm 139:13–16).

Because trauma, grief, and loss all get stored in our bodies, discharging it is vital. What does that even mean? Discharge includes movement and verbal processing. Each person may discharge differently based on their personality, background, and experiences. Some may gravitate toward physical releases such as deep tissue massage, running, or horseback riding, while others will move toward drama, music, art, or writing poetry. It is imperative that you find what works for you. I used to keep a mini-trampoline in my office and invited anyone that needed to discharge to come into my office and jump because jumping changes the brain. Try it when you find yourself stuck in problem-solving. Also, walking is a great option because it creates bi-lateral stimulation so that both sides of the brain begin to work with each other. When both sides of the brain are engaged, the creative side can soar, thus, innovation builds new ideas and solutions.

I am a verbal processor, so often find that I discharge through meeting with others, usually over food or something warm to drink, and then spending time talking through whatever is on our minds. I value relationships and find them to be vital in my processing efforts. You know your discharge works when you experience a sense of relief, a place of calm, or an insight. This balance keeps us in a state where we can grow, learn, and connect. It's important to release our emotional content and experiences regularly, so try to build it into your daily, weekly, or even monthly disciplines. I find when I don't do this that I am more irritable and my focus can be compromised. My verbal processing with friends may include hilarious laughter, a few tears or even moments of sobbing and anything in-between.

Rather than talk therapy, you might benefit from running,

drumming, journaling, singing, humming, dancing, throwing, or other activities. The visceral release that comes from activity helps to move the trauma, grief, or loss out of the body, not letting it take root, resulting in various disruptive behaviors or emotions. Now while this is very important to understand for yourself, it is also vital to be aware of for those you are leading. You may see their fears show up in unlikely ways. They may freeze up and become indecisive. They might show up as whiny or needy. They could also become argumentative or defensive if they feel challenged or misunderstood. And fear can also show up as trying to appease or please others to stay safe and unnoticed. If you are aware of these possibilities, you can respond to your staff, giving them what they need to feel safe, seen and heard. When you do that, you create trust. When we work in an environment of trust, we can engage in creative and innovative endeavors. Can you create scripts or code words for discharge options? Can you say, "Is this a walking moment?" or can we ask if someone needs to take a moment? How can you make it okay for others to ask for what they need? Can you model this for your teams, your leaders, and yourself?

James 5:16 states that if we confess our sins and pray for each other, we will be healed. Confessing our sins is a form of discharge; we are releasing our sins. Be prudent about who you confess to, but don't neglect doing this. There is great relief when we unload the burden that sin creates in our lives. When we release it, God forgives, and we need to forgive ourselves. Then our sin is as far away as the east is from the west. That, my friends, creates healing of our souls. This is God's desire for us. For me, this is living in God's best for my life. For in this we will find peace, the peace that passes all understanding.

Debi Grebenik, Ph.D.

Step into unpacking shame

The definition of shame is best captured by Brené Brown : "Shame is an intensely painful feeling or experience of believing that we are flawed and therefor unworthy of love and belonging." https://brenebrown.com/articles/2013/01/15/shame-v-guilt/

Shame comes from the place where you believe that you aren't enough; that you may never be enough. Shame is different than guilt or embarrassment. Guilt and embarrassment are because of something you did or said. Shame is exacerbated by silence, secrecy, and judgment.

The antidote to shame is empathy. Empathy is the ability to feel someone else's pain or shame. Empathy is the ability to sit with another in their distress, particularly without giving advice or trying to fix them. When we receive empathy for something that brought us shame, the shame can dissipate. Think of a time when you did something that created shame in your life, if you called your friend and they communicated judgment to you, your shame would grow exponentially. If that same friend were to say they were so sorry that you were going through your experience, your shame would begin to fade away. Remember, we need compassion when we feel shameful, and we can give compassion when others feel shame. Be aware of how shame may show up in your life. Another important ingredient needed to dissipate shame is forgiveness—self-forgiveness and the ultimate forgiveness that only comes from God the Father who gives it freely.

God never intended for us to live in shame. Genesis 2:25 says that "The man and his wife were both naked, and they felt no shame." Only because of Satan's lies did shame enter into our experience. And shame changes us, it can create isolation and keep us from becoming our best selves.

My shame story runs deep and began when I was born to a teenage mother in the 1950s. She was forced to drop out of high school and never received her high school diploma. She missed out on all the teenage activities. Judgment and shame were the responses of her peers, family, and other adults in her life. She was advised to abort me to avoid the shame being hurled at her. Her shame infused all that she did and all that she was. That was passed on to me and I spent most of my life trying to be worthy of all she experienced during her pregnancy. My response was to try and perform, to excel, believing that if I earned enough degrees or honors, I would finally be worthy enough of all the shame and loss she experienced from being an unwed teen mother in the 1950s. Shame and perfectionism seem to be partners in causing us to feel defeated. Find people in your life who will give you bountiful amounts of empathy and compassion so you can work through your own shame stories. Those people are your people and are worth the investment to build relationships with them. Understanding my mom's shame story, helped to illuminate mine and create opportunities for my own healing. I never understood why I always felt a relentless burning in my belly to achieve and pursue academic pursuits. The pieces were starting to fit together. I also witnessed my mom at my doctoral graduation and hooding. She reveled in my success and celebrated me. This helped to temper my drive for achievement and to rest in who I am and who God created me to be.

Shame keeps us from being vulnerable. Talk to that small circle of people that you trust completely. Be vulnerable; invite them into your story. Let them see your shame. If they don't give you the compassion you need, find others who will. Don't fear vulnerability. As we are vulnerable, others respond with their own stories. Then we will be in the position to give grace and compassion. This group should be small—the people you invite in need to earn the invitation to be in your inner circle. Some that you invite in may not pass the test, they may violate your trust. Be prepared for this and know that you can create boundaries about who you let in your life as well as boundaries about what you share and with whom.

About now, you are probably wondering about how all this fits into the workplace. Whether we acknowledge it or not, our emotions and trauma histories show up in our work settings. Your colleagues may shut down, be hypersensitive, or even display anger. These responses are very similar to trauma responses. We tend to only look at the behaviors rather than trying to figure out the why behind the behavior. We don't need to be a therapist to understand some of the reactions. Most people I know and worked with did not intend to show up in disruptive ways—they were experiencing unprocessed pain, trauma, or shame. Knowing this helps us keep perspective and avoid judging.

Shame also shows up in the workplace through our teams' feelings of unworthiness. These feelings can cause us to freeze up, be indecisive, or even to isolate. When our team members isolate, silos may result which keeps us from working effectively or inefficiently. The sense of unworthiness can also demand a significant amount of emotional energy to manage. Be aware of this and compassionately provide opportunities for those who are struggling to get the support they need and deserve. The support may need to be provided by an external source-through coaching or even therapy. Earlier we talked about psychological safety which means that we are seen, heard, and valued. If and when we can create psychological safety for our teams, unworthiness can dissipate because team members are able to connect to their value. Sometimes when others sense we see their value, they can take that in and begin to believe in their own worthiness. While this is difficult, it is not impossible. We can speak truth into others by sharing how we see them and by acknowledging their super powers. I try to do this for those with whom I work. Recently I initiated a conversation about what LLCs (Limited Liability Corporations) others could create. I took my turn and shared with each one the potential and gifts I saw in them. It was a time of laughter, tempered by truth-saying.

Here is a diagram that identifies the importance of building psychological safety as foundational.

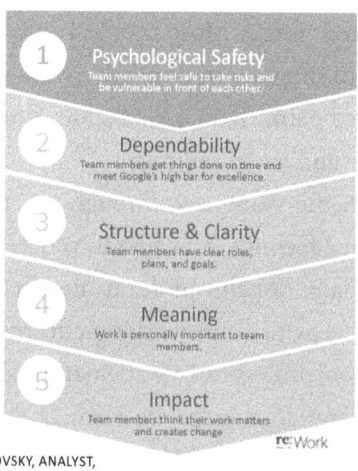

JULIA ROZOVSKY, ANALYST,
GOOGLE PEOPLE OPERATIONS
NOVEMBER 17, 2015

Sometimes we want to move to impact before we secure the foundational elements of psychological safety, dependability, structure and clarity, meaning and then impact grows out of those building blocks. Dependability helps to build relational trust which allows for innovation and creativity. Structure and clarity provide the vehicle to deliver trust so that teams can work together effectively and efficiently. Meaning emerges once the basic blocks are put in place. Impact is the desired outcome and worthy of the work to create.

The goal is to move from being full of shame to being free of shame. It is a process and healing is only possible through relationships that give grace, forgiveness, and empathy. Take the time work through your own shame story. Make the unseen seen. Build up others' fortitude so that they can do this important work for themselves.

Here are 5 ways you can address shame:

1. Listen to your body; it will speak to you.
2. Take time to reflect on your past, your pain, and your purpose.
3. Find someone you trust to share your shame with. Isolation is the fertilizer for depression and unworthiness. Finding our worthiness is required for emotional healing.
4. Seek additional help if needed.
5. Reflect if any of your past might be considered traumatic. Get additional help if needed.

Don't react

Remember that trauma may cause reactions that do not seem to fit the situation. When you see this occur, it will take an extra measure of self-awareness and self-regulation to not react. Try to respond from a place of love and compassion. We may not love a particular person, yet we can be firmly grounded in responses that are loving. Loving ways are outlined in I Corinthians 13 and include:

- Patience
- Kindness
- Does not envy
- Is not proud
- Is not rude
- Does not boast
- Is not self-seeking
- Is not easily angered
- Keeps no record of wrongs
- Does not delight in evil
- Rejoices with the truth
- Always protects
- Always trusts
- Always hopes
- Always perseveres

These attributes create loving responses which builds connection and safety. Compassionate accountability is a useful tool when someone on your team reacts in a way that seems difficult to understand.

I observed several incidents that surprised me as a supervisor and leader. At times, I reacted out of frustration, partly because I was upset about how some of my staff's behaviors or choices may reflect on my work or reputation. I was insecure enough that I was worried that others would see me as incompetent if my staff were less than perfect. I can see the fallacy in this type of thinking yet at the time my anxiety was real. Only when I was calm and regulated was I able to respond in a way that stayed true to my values. Keep in the forefront that your goal can be to **_do what love would do_**.

Since we know that God is love, this is basically another way of saying that we need to do what God would want us to do.

Let me illustrate this principle in action. Several years ago, I witnessed a staff member going to court inebriated. I knew the person was suffering from depression. While I still needed to terminate the person, I stated that I hoped they would be able to take some time to seek healing and help to process their feelings. This is such a hard process; we can show up with compassion, tempered with accountability. The staff member responded to my calm approach, and we averted an angry or emotional outburst. I felt as though I dealt with a difficult situation in a way that honored and lived up to my values.

Move through

When we lead with a sense of purpose, we need courage to step into that purpose. It is easy to stay where you are rather than to move into where you want to go and who you want to be. The proofing of your purpose comes from moving through the difficulties and growth opportunities to find your zone. The learning comes as we *move through*. When we get overwhelmed, we can feel stuck and stop moving. Try to accept the lessons you will learn during the struggle, so you don't need to repeat the same process. Think of geese, they fly in formation with one goose in the lead. As the first goose tires, they move back into the formation until they are ready to take the lead again. They don't quit, they just take a moment and share the responsibility with others. This doesn't mean they are weak, it identifies their needs and how they act to meet them. Their formation is intact and they get to where they set out to go—we should copy this strategy.

If you find yourself feeling stuck, talk to someone who can help you process and clarify what might be going on for you. I coach multiple leaders, and most of what I do is validate their process and help them to clarify what to do with their emotions, fears, and anxieties. As we verbally process, I provide insights and let them reflect on them to determine how they want to proceed. It is important that, as a coach, I just guide their process without being directive. It is incredibly valuable to invite someone into your journey to provide perspective, support, and insight. Sometimes it is very difficult to see what is going on when we are so intimately involved. Additionally, we may not want to see what is happening because we aren't ready to deal with the fallout or the changes required. It is exciting to be at the place where you can look back and see all that you learned. Don't rush through the process. Savor the journey. And remember to take time to reflect on your learning and growth or you may miss where you came from and potentially where you are going. Chart your progress, missteps and all.

Steps you can take

Think through your own trauma history. Be aware of your background and any traumatic experiences you went through. If you aren't sure what trauma is or if you experienced it, answer the ten questions on this website: www.acestoohigh.com. The questions compile the adverse childhood events that contribute to trauma. If you score a four or above, you might want to consider engaging in trauma work. I highly recommend EMDR (Eye-movement desensitization reprocessing) as an effective trauma clinical strategy. Trauma-focused yoga, art or music therapy or journaling/narrative work can also be beneficial. Find what works for you. Do your research. I don't recommend cognitive work until you engage in experiential work.

Include any experiences that caused you harm or that impacted your emotional wellbeing or relationships. Don't be afraid to call them trauma. If we can name what it is then we can tame its impact. You get to define what impacted you-for each of that it can look different so we aren't to judge others' experiences.

Consider how trauma is stored in your body. Pay attention to your body; identify pains, aches, or other somatic symptoms. Explore tightness or any sensory responses. Sometimes a particular smell may evoke a memory or emotional reaction. For example, the smell of warm cookies reminds me of my mom's baking. Be aware of how you or your staff may be activated by sensory memories and you won't see it coming. Sensory response are activated by something we smell, hear, touch, taste or see. Is your jaw tense? Does your head hurt? Is your stomach nauseated? These might be signals that there is something in your body that is not processed. For example, you may be experiencing headaches because something from your past is difficult to get your head around. Or perhaps you can't stomach something so your stomach is aching. Remember to look for the metaphor in the behavior, aches, and discomfort.

Reflect on your family's trauma history; their history impacts your physiology. This might be a time to ask a family member if there were any traumatic events in the family that you might not be aware of. I will never forget the conversations with my mother when she told me about losing her mother to cancer when she was only eight years of age. She shared visceral memories with me, and I could feel her pain and loss. That shaped her story for the rest of her life. It helped me understand some of the choices and reactions of her life. Ask the hard questions; they might help you to gain insight and wisdom into your own history, emotions, pain, and reactions.

Find consistent ways to build discharge activities into your everyday life. Find discharge activities that fit your personality, interests, and needs. Be creative and follow through with your ideas. Practice these activities consistently. We can't really wait until we need the discharge to do it; we need to stay current with our discharge so that our emotional distress doesn't build up and become toxic.

Seek to understand how shame shows up in your life. Give empathy to others who may be caught in their own shame spirals. Be aware that shame sneaks up on you and may tend to be all-consuming. Our shame can isolate us and prevent us from connecting with others. When we share with others (a select few), we can experience some freedom and relief as we connect over our humanness.

Try to avoid blaming—yourself and others. Realize that your tendency to blame may be related to your sense of being overwhelmed. Blaming pulls us apart rather than creating connection. Remember that our goal in leadership is building relational connections from which we can lead. How we show up is what builds safe and effective relationships-the foundation of leadership efficacy.

Avoid getting stuck; keep moving. Remember that moving through is where the learning occurs.

Take time to work on yourself. Seek out professional help if you think that might be helpful; whether that is therapy, coaching, a sabbatical or other strategies.

Engage a coach or colleague to help guide your process. Be open to hearing feedback from someone who earned your trust. Don't fear the process. Elevate learning as your goal. Enter the process wholeheartedly as that is where the growth will occur.

CHAPTER 3

Why are we talking about fear?

Step through fear

We can't understand leadership without looking at fear. Fears abound; however, "perfect love casts out all fear" (I John 4:18). And guess where we can find perfect love? Only in God the Father can we find the perfect love that we desire, need, and seek. Even the Scripture gives weight to fear. Throughout the Old and New Testaments, we can read about fears of individuals, of God, and of judgment. The fears range from God seeing our sins to God not seeing us or even the fear of not enough food or water. God uses the phrase "Fear not" frequently throughout the Bible. The fears are real, and we can't just ignore them or shove them aside.

What do you think of when we talk about fear? Fear of spiders, of flying, of heights? Or do you think of the fear of failure, the fear of being alone, the fear of dying, or even the overwhelming fear of being found out? Are you afraid that others may determine that you don't really know what you are doing? Some call this the "imposter syndrome": you feel incompetent and are afraid that others will find out. And then what would you do? Isn't that fear the fear of being seen for who we are, full of flaws? And what would happen if we were fully seen? That would make us vulnerable.

Fear can wreak havoc on your emotions, increase your anxiety, and impair your judgment—not a good recipe for effective leadership. Fear is at the root of so many emotions and behaviors because it causes dysregulation. Dysregulation occurs when our equilibrium is upset. Think of it this way; calm is the desired state. We are cruising along then something or someone comes along to disrupt our calm. It may be that someone is critical of you, or maybe a new initiative that you developed failed, or perhaps you find yourself doubting your decisions. How fast you leave your calm can be a direct result of your background and experiences. If your background includes trauma, you might find yourself responding emotionally—perhaps in ways you didn't imagine.

Think of it this way, your supervisor sees you in the hall and says, "I need to talk to you." Immediately you go to a place of fear and think *Oh my, what did I do wrong this time?* or *They finally figured out that I don't know what I'm doing.* That is fear speaking. Your fear shuts you down and keeps you from being present and showing up as your best self. Fear, when left free to rein, can cause significant devastation. Living in fear is not part of God's design for us. Once again, when we name it for what it is, we can tame it so that it doesn't control us, changing our outcome from fear to freedom.

Step into self-awareness

Self-awareness helps to take the power out of fear. When we can acknowledge our fears and their impact, we can trust God with them. Many of our fears are based on lies from Satan. As our self-awareness grows, we can dismantle the lies and replace them with truth. When we come from a place where we are firmly rooted in truth, lies can't survive. Truth brings light and dispels Satan's darkness. Lies cause us to armor up—to protect—and to hide. Armor protects us, not letting anything in, and it also prevents anything from getting out. When we are armored up, we can't connect with others which impedes our ability to lead. Armor can serve a purpose in certain situations; however, if we maintain it, it may outlive its benefit and purpose.

Other ways fear can show up include depression, anger, or disassociation. Fear breeds defensiveness because we are afraid of what will happen if others can see our fear or anxiety. Being seen creates vulnerability, and many of us are not interested in being vulnerable. To be seen is very scary. One of our greatest needs is to be seen and heard. And in contrast, one of our greatest fears is to be seen and heard.

Think of Psalm 139 which says, "Search me, God, and know my heart; test me and know my anxious thoughts." This verse is clear; it doesn't suggest that God should check to see if I think any anxious thoughts—God assumes that our anxious thoughts are there. This gives me great hope. We are to ask God to know our heart. We do not need to approach Him from a place of fear or shame; it is part of His plan to be known. And when we are known by our Heavenly Father and can celebrate His acceptance of us, then we can move toward being known by others. Then vulnerability isn't quite so scary.

What? I can hear you right now. You don't want others to know of your anxieties, your insecurities, and your fears. I get it. It's hard to be vulnerable and transparent. Maybe others won't want to follow or trust you. Or maybe they will. Who do you want to follow? Someone with it all together or someone you can relate to with their humanness, flaws, and imperfections? I thought that if I presented myself as being all together all the time, others would want to follow. Yet when I looked behind me, no one was there. So it wasn't a far jump to realize that if no one is following, then we can't really call ourselves leaders.

When I began to show up as vulnerable, owning my mistakes and imperfections, others began to relate and subsequently follow me. This is the opposite of how I thought things would work. I wanted others to see me as being confident, strong, and whatever additional positive adjective you want to add. Yet, in my weakness, God made me strong. God is so good at equipping us when we allow Him to fill us up. My heart's desire is for more of Him, less of me. To do this requires me to quit making things about me and letting God's wisdom, peace, and light shine through me. This takes a daily practice of asking God for His power rather than leaning on myself. The key word here is "practice." And those things that we practice we improve.

Here are 5 ways that you can address fear:

1. Acknowledge the presence of your fear. Once again self-awareness is vital.
2. Pay attention to where fear resides in your body. Sometimes we need to sit with it and feel all the feels before we can move through it.
3. Pay attention to how your past may be creating your current fears. Ask God to show you any unresolved concerns that might be contributing to or building your fears.

4. Find ways to discharge your emotional content. We already discussed and gave you multiple options to discharge.
5. Talk about fear with others as fear is a shared human experience. Find those you can process with so you can be validated in your journey.

Step into your past

Also, important to note is that your fears may be due to unprocessed trauma, grief, or loss. Sometimes we are unaware of the imprint past experiences leave on us. And if we didn't process or discharge the pain from our early incidents, then fear, anxiety, or other emotional responses may develop. Our bodies store our pain and it seeps out, preventing us from becoming the person we want and that God created us to be. Rather than stuffing our pain, we can start with an awareness of our history's impact on our emotions. Therapy might be an option to work through some challenges. Many people find journaling, meditation, prayer, and reflection to be helpful. I really can't emphasize this enough-it is a repetitive theme that needs to be addressed. When things are repeated, the message is that it is something important to note.

If you notice a reaction that doesn't make sense, pause, and realize that your colleague may not be intentionally acting out. They may be overwhelmed by their emotions and lack the self-awareness to identify the cause of their distress. They also may not be able to regulate their emotions. We may not know what is driving their behavior; yet we can let them know that we are not standing in judgment and are willing to give them what they need to process through their distress. Just acknowledging this can help others to find their sense of calm again. Part of leadership is staying regulated enough so that we can see things that others can't. You need to keep your lamp full so that you can help to light others' lamps.

Step into insight

I was coaching an executive leader recently who was talking about her inability to make decisions out of her fear of messing up or not getting it right. She told me that she needed to collect all the data she could, research every option, and then think deeply about how to respond before deciding. This process showed up in both her personal and professional lives. It was debilitating. She didn't really like being this way yet couldn't figure out how to change this pattern.

As we began to unpack what was going on with her, I asked her if I could share my observations with her. She agreed and I shared that perhaps she was frozen in shame. Indecisiveness is symptomatic of shame. She was confused and couldn't connect the dots. As we discussed this further, she admitted that she never felt good enough as a leader. She doubted her decision-making abilities and her judgment. As she processed, she began to see that shame enveloped her, keeping her from showing up as confident or as the leader she yearned to be. I sat with her in her newfound discovery. I didn't offer advice, didn't try to fix her, and just let her think and feel all her feelings—something we don't often like to do because it is uncomfortable and unpredictable.

At our next coaching session, she seemed very eager and somewhat impatient. I asked her what was going on and she stated that our last session changed her life (her words, not mine).

She further explained that understanding the impact of shame on her life helped put the pieces of her puzzle together to form a picture that resonated with her. She now knew why she couldn't make decisions, why she second-guessed herself, and even why she was afraid of others' opinions of her. She was ecstatic with this new awareness and felt that she was already becoming a different leader. Her 'aha moment' was significant in its impact. She remarked that even others noticed a difference in her. They saw a newfound confidence in her and a willingness to step into decisions. When our confidence grows, others see us as more competent. Interestingly, when our competence grows, our confidence blossoms.

When we know better, we can do better. When shame lives in us, we often tell stories that we aren't enough, that we aren't worthy. Because of our sense of unworthiness, we respond from a place of fear without wanting to risk failing. These fears cause us to fight, take flight, or freeze. These are maladaptive leadership responses. This coaching client stayed in a freeze response where she couldn't make decisions. Once we build our self-awareness, we can determine what to change, build, or adapt. When we make the commitment to change, we might need someone to coach or support our journey. Leadership coaching may be a good option for you as you seek to become the leader God purposed you to be. Sometimes our wisdom comes from a rearview look at our experiences, mistakes, and lessons learned.

Step into putting the puzzle together

I was coaching another woman recently and we were working on her personal and professional development. I used the metaphor of a puzzle with her. I suggested that we start by looking at all the pieces on the table. The pieces symbolized who she was at that moment and the finish puzzle created the picture of who she wanted to be. And as we assembled those pieces, we constructed a picture, a puzzle that was greater than the sum of the pieces. That's the beauty of taking time, reflecting, and investing in your self-awareness, goals, and dreams. This is such an exciting journey to go on for ourselves and with others. I look forward to hearing about her self-discovery journey. I reminded her to let go of her need to control the outcome and to trust the process. This is where we pray for wisdom and for the Holy Spirit to show us truth and insight. She continues to find additional pieces and continues to revise the picture she wants to create.

It appears I collect puzzle pieces all the time as I am learning daily. While collecting the pieces, I experience several "aha moments" of my own and still need to experience a few more. I wish I could say that I moved on a straight path toward greatness. The real story is that just last week I found myself apologizing for something I said. Yes, even at my age I am still saying things that don't build up or give grace. I am still learning how to bridle my mouth. I thought I could just coast at this stage in my life; however, mistakes are still part of my everyday existence. Fortunately, I am good at apologizing because I've practiced a lot. I wish I didn't give myself so much to work with; I wish I got things right the first time instead of the $43,256^{th}$ time (or so it seems). I grimace at even writing these words down here. I even want you, the reader, to see me in a positive light! And yet, apologies build connections because they require humility, compassion, and forgiveness.

Debi Grebenik, Ph.D.

Step into vulnerability

My first venture into vulnerability began very tentatively. I tiptoed into it. I misunderstood what it was, so it took me awhile to figure it all out. And I am still figuring it out. Vulnerability is not oversharing or telling intimate details of my life. It is the process of showing up as my truest, most authentic self. I saw this in such a powerful way on a cold January day in 2012. My mom was very ill with cancer and in an ICU, and on that day her sister called me from the hospital in the city where I grew up. My mom decided to stop all medical interventions. She was ready to die, that day, and I was 600 miles away. I was devastated. I called my leadership team together and told them of this news and asked for their help and support. They actually made a circle around me and said, "We got you. We got this[the work]." It was beautiful, and I felt their love and support.

I got there in time to say good-bye, and my mom died that day. I returned to the office three days later. I told my staff that I may struggle, and if they saw my office door closed, I was taking a moment. I didn't need to go into details, I just let them know I wasn't doing well. That was the first time I ever expressed complete vulnerability. There was no control over the situation and that was difficult. In my openness I was able to receive the care and nurturing so freely offered to me. This experience marked me, lighting the pathway of vulnerability for me. It also opened my ability to connect with others in their grief, loss, and pain. Their support helped me in the days, weeks, and even months ahead as I was starting my grief journey.

My sense of being a leader wasn't compromised. In fact, I

believe that when my humanness was so evident, others wanted to connect with me and weren't afraid to share their own vulnerability. Their willingness to share was the biggest positive outcome to appear from my openness.

I also learned that admitting I didn't know something was another element of showing up as vulnerable. My understanding of leadership was certainly shifting. I still wanted to prove my abilities because that was what fit my definition of being an effective leader.

I couldn't really find anyone to talk with about all these thoughts and emotions. Yet, I noticed that things were shifting at my job—the culture was catching on to this new way of work and staff were responding positively to increased vulnerability and transparency. They subsequently began sharing their own fears. Maybe we were unleashing our potential. We began to find our creative and innovative muscles. We were building momentum. When you think of the word "vulnerability," do you shudder, or do you seek to embrace it? What is your experience with vulnerability? Was it positive or negative?

The momentum was continuing to build, and I was excited because I am wired for novelty and adventure. I operated from a place of *ready, fire, aim*. Leading change is a skill that many leaders may not even think about. I realized that once again I was getting ready for another growth spurt. I thought if I just stepped forward with new programming, everyone would simply follow my lead. You may find yourself laughing at me now, and I wouldn't blame you. I'm laughing as I write this.

I discovered Reflective Supervision which is based on a different type of relating to those you supervise. We began implementing these concepts into our supervision and began to reap the results. Our staff were responding to the strategies because we were noticing more. As leaders we might start our supervision with comments such as I observed that during a conversation you seemed reluctant to participate or somewhat stressed. Then we leave space for them to respond. The staff tested the waters on sharing how they really felt and were met with compassion and connection rather than judgment or correction. Shifting to this type of supervision created a 'connect before you correct' philosophy.

Step into change

Leading change requires paying attention to the pace of change. Something that I never realized before is that we develop a relationship with change—some of us embrace it, some shun it, and some reluctantly accept it. It is vital that leaders lead at a pace their staff can tolerate. This is another area where self-awareness is paramount. We need to realize how our past experiences shape our responses to change.

I remember a time when I was so excited to expand into new programming and I was explaining my ideas to the leadership team. In response, one of the leaders said, "You know Debi, I think we need to slow down. We need to work on some of our current programs before we bring anything new on." These were not words I wanted to hear, and yet, I listened. This leader was closer to the actual work than I was, so they were better informed about the pace we needed to work from. We didn't pursue the new opportunity. Instead, we focused on current programming which resulted in positioning us perfectly for a new program about six months later. It is important that we listen and manage our change efforts so that our staff continue to follow.

The next lesson I learned about change was the need to address the loss that occurred. Change includes loss—loss of consistency, loss of comfort, loss of confidence, and loss of competence. We can acknowledge losses by naming and validating that they occurred. We can also create a ritual to mark the spot where an ending happened while giving opportunity for staff to express their feelings about the changes. These alterations may also include loss of a title, reputation, way of work, or position.

A specific ending helps to provide clarity. For example, when getting ready to eliminate a particular procedure, we can state that we will use the current format until the beginning of the next month. This gives a specific ending time.

Another part of change to manage is the in-between time or the neutral zone nestled in the middle of the old way and the new way, which is considered the messy middle. Confusion can easily settle in when staff aren't aware if they are operating in the old way or in the new way. As leaders, we need to over-communicate which will pave the way to trusting and following you. This is also a time when leaders can hold space for their teams to process their emotions and to not be okay. For example, leaders can validate the challenges imbedded in the change process, acknowledge the multiple unknowns in the process, and even express empathy for the duress being experienced.

When leaders don't show up with advice, with a fix-it mentality, or with a shaming/blaming response, then the staff are more able to process all they are going through. We all need time to reflect and think about what we're experiencing. I'm sure you've experienced the situation where someone tried to implement change without a clear ending or a distinct beginning. The confusion that results is very disorienting and can create significant levels of stress. Leaders should hold the space for those working through the change.

Step into gaining perspective

When change happens, we may feel a loss of control. This is when you need to step back and get out of the fray so that you can recapture your perspective. Think of it as the authors Marty Linsky and Ronald Heifetz of *Leadership on the Line* illustrate when they say to step off the dance floor and onto the balcony to change your vantage point. The balcony allows us to see the bigger picture and all the pieces that we may be missing when we are in the middle of the dance floor. Be aware of where you are in the moment. Do you need to change your view? Do you need to get another vantage point? What would it take to leave the known to visit the unknown?

Then be mindful about all components of the change process; the pace of the change, the emotional content of those in the change, the anxiety accompanying the process, and the climate of the organization during the change. This is really the fun part and includes robust content for our work. Lean into this and learn to harvest the good stuff.

Another feature of leading change is to keep the vision of where you are going at the forefront of decision-making. Make sure that all your staff can articulate your vision. It's important for everyone to know where they are going so they are willing to stay the course during the change process. It is also imperative to understand our individual purpose or why. We are motivated and driven by our purpose. Simon Sinek is a British-American author and inspirational speaker who wrote the best-selling book *Start with Why*, and he tells us to start with our personal *why*. The *why* is not how or what we do, rather it's why we get up in the morning or why we want to make a difference. When we can connect our purpose to the mission or vision of the organization where we work, we will feel energized and resilient. Therefore, I am still excited to get to do the work that I am doing. I am working from a place of my *why*—my purpose—and find myself in my zone. This is another strategy that builds and promotes resilience, particularly when the work becomes hard or unpredictable.

Building resilience is vital. Burnout is one element of compassion fatigue. It is associated with feelings of hopelessness and difficulties in dealing with work or in working effectively. If we don't attend to these symptoms we are actually contributing to burnout. Pay attention to your staff that seem overwhelmed all of the time or that are missing work often because they are calling sick. Also attend to those who are experiencing chronic stress. Be aware of the role their trauma histories may play in their ability to navigate stress. Workforce wellbeing is an important aspiration and relates to all aspects of working life, from the quality and safety of the physical environment, to how workers feel about their work, the climate at work and the commitment to organizational purpose. The goal is to make sure workers are safe, healthy, satisfied, and engaged at work. Building resilience in individuals and within the organization addresses wellbeing. Keep this as a priority in your work. We can't give what we don't have.

Resilience also builds the capacity to bend without breaking. Think of palm trees, their roots are deep and strong. Their strong root system allows them to bend during strong winds without breaking. Consider how we can build strong root systems in ourselves, our staff, and our organizations. An important consideration in building wellbeing is to determine how to instill expectations of rest. Are you communicating that acceptance only comes with performance or are you able to recognize and reinforce that the pace of our work is significant. We are humans who need rest and leaders can set the tone that rest is acceptable. Rest includes taking your vacations, being off after work hours and during weekends.

Think of ways you can build rest into your organization:

_____

_____

_____

_____

Leaders set the culture for wellbeing. They sanction the allocation of resources to attend to wellbeing. They role model their own wellbeing practices. They also identify and remove systemic barriers to wellbeing practices. You might say that leaders are ambassadors of wellbeing. As you build these practices, you will find that your staff will want to stay; they will begin to appreciate what it is that you provide and prioritize.

Just Show Up

Our teams must know that they are valued. If they feel that their work is valued, this contributes to their wellbeing and commitment to stay the course in their positions. Another strategy is to make sure that employees feel included decisions, strategy development and successes. When our staff feel part of something bigger than themselves, they feel contentment and a sense of wellbeing. Clarity of roles and job expectations also helps to build a culture of wellbeing.

Additionally, workloads must be reasonable enough to complete so that a balance of work and living can be created and maintained. Make sure that the implicit messages are the same as the explicit ones. Sometimes we say one thing and yet the culture supports something else. We may say that we think everyone should take time for lunch or take their vacations; then we don't provide coverage when our teammates are off. The message is mixed and confusing, creating stress and uncertainty. With prolonged stress, dissatisfaction will increase. Another good tool you can use is to give stay interviews quarterly or randomly. You don't need to interview everyone; you can set up a system to select participants randomly.

Questions to include might be:
- What do you like most about your job?
- What would you like to change about your position?
- What causes you stress?
- What would cause you to leave your position?
- What keeps you here?
- What do we need to do more of?
- Less of?

The data from these questions can be very useful in changing course or building in new practices. Pay attention to the information you receive.

Part of what I find fulfilling is to guide others in finding their purpose by asking thoughtful questions. My *why* is to help others connect the dots of their personal and professional lives. My hope is that we can all find our own zones of spiritual giftedness and skills, experience, and talents which will help us stay the course. As you coach and lead others, be aware that it is easy to be derailed, to lose sight of the goal, or to be so distracted that you never get to where you intend. This can be a very subtle detour and significant in its impact. Knowing your *why* can help you to maintain your focus and keep your goal in mind.

Feeling supported is also an important variable in creating a wellbeing-focused culture. Knowing that someone "has their back" creates a sense of safety and belonging. Supervision is provided consistently and includes ongoing feedback so that a spirit of transparency is evident. The team all know where they stand, what they are rocking and what they need to work on. The spirit of transparency builds integrity, trust, and safety. It also creates predictability which helps those with trauma histories. Accountability is part of the transparency as staff are held accountable to outcomes. They are held to personal responsibility and self-determination to the extent that their position allows.

Successes are celebrated. We may need to be creative about what the successes are. You might practice a high five Friday, good news Monday, shout outs to recognize staff performance, dance parties, serious and sill awards, thank you notes or other recognitions. Staff also need to feel that their work aligns to a common vision which creates a sense of belonging and wellbeing. When we feel that we belong, that our successes are seen, and that wellbeing is highlighted, staff members are more likely to contribute in meaningful ways building retention.

Name some ways you can celebrate successes:

_____

_____

_____

_____

What are ways we can express value to our team members:

_____

_____

_____

_____

Debi Grebenik, Ph.D.

Step through, not around

Sometimes our fear keeps us from difficult conversations or confrontations. It is important to understand that we can't avoid or dodge these. In my career, unfortunately, I terminated more people than I ever imagined would be necessary. This was after giving them multiple opportunities to grow and improve. I also counseled many people out of their positions; I knew it wasn't a good fit for them in their current positions and, at some level, they did too. These were not conversations I ever thought I would initiate, and what I realized is that for some staff it was a relief. With my support and a positive reference, they felt seen and heard in a way that they could make the difficult choice to make the difficult decision of leaving. It is important that we not avoid these challenging conversations just because they are uncomfortable. Sometimes pushing through the difficult topics creates opportunities for growth and can be freeing.

Other conversations I didn't ever intend to engage in included confronting drinking during working hours, someone making racist remarks, or unprofessional behavior such as eye-rolling during meetings with external project partners. What I learned by my willingness to address these behaviors is that others could see that I was attending to behaviors that affected the culture. A sense of safety resulted as staff knew that inappropriate behaviors would not be tolerated. I didn't realize that people needed to see that leaders weren't afraid to address performance issues. While it wasn't comfortable, I learned to address situations head-on with calm, kindness, and grace. I also figured out that when these difficult conversations occurred, it was easy to say too much so I tried to state succinctly what was observed and what needed to happen. The culture of any organization is created by the worst behavior the leader is willing to tolerate. Know what you will or will not tolerate and communicate this clearly to your entire team. These are the guardrails that will guide your staff coaching and supervision.

I coached other supervisors who needed to address performance issues to do the same. I also volunteered to be present with them when engaging in one of those dreaded conversations because I knew how nervous they were. For some of us with trauma backgrounds, we may seek peace at all costs and avoid confrontation. I hear your pain, reluctance, and even your fear—fear of messing it up, fear of being challenged, fear of retaliation, or any number of fears. This is where your element of calm is required; take a deep breath, leave your door slightly open, let someone know what you are doing, and plan to debrief afterwards through a walk or talk with a trusted colleague. We need to be willing to do the hard things because we will repeat what we don't repair. Remember that the growth happens when we repair what we rupture. Sometimes we are stronger after the rupture than we were before it happened.

Step into power

Only when we realize that our power as leaders is not to be used to coerce or persuade others can we use influence to motivate others to find their way. When we use influence, we can take others from the known to the unknown as we support them in this scary part of their journey. Many people only think of power as a negative; however, power can create influence and change to accomplish goals. The dark side of power is when it is used to coerce or control others. We also need to think about power differentials and be aware of how those impact those without perceived power.

We hold onto our old ways for a variety of reasons that include believing that we must stay in our comfort zone, our mentor taught us to do it this way, it's working, or I am afraid of something different. In response, we fight to preserve the known. We work hard to maintain the familiar, to restore order, and as a result, we create resistance. With trauma histories in our past, we may find ourselves addicted to sameness and predictability. Power is neither positive nor negative, it's how it is used that determines its impact so let's use it to build up others. And let's identify its existence in the room or situation that we find ourselves.

Steps to work through fear and manage change

1. Acknowledge your fear. Name it to tame it. Fears are common to all of us. When we name our fears, they lose some of their power. Remember that perfect love (love from God our Father) casts out all fear.

2. Lean into vulnerability; embrace what it brings to your work and relationships. Understand what vulnerability is and what it isn't. Encourage others to be vulnerable with you. Be that safe person for them. Give them the gift of your trust.

3. Hold space for those who are experiencing change and transitions. Let them process without judgment. Stay away from trying to fix; stay with them and let them know it's okay to not be okay.

4. Don't be afraid of difficult conversations. Learn the art

of how to manage conflict, challenges, and confrontations. These skills can be developed and practiced. Approach these conversations with humility, kindness, and gentleness.

5. Work on your own self-awareness; know what activates you and what you need to do to maintain your calm.

6. Pray for wisdom and insights. God will answer this prayer. He wants to give us what we need; all we need to do is ask.

7. Don't underestimate the impact of fear—yours and those you lead. The fears may originate from early development, professional experience, previous traumas, or all the above. The fear is real and not to be dismissed or mocked. Support others as they identify and push through their fears.

8. Understand that fear shows up in a variety of responses. Don't react out of your own anxiety; pause and seek understanding of what might be motivating your fear response and the response of those you supervise.

9. Take care of yourself during these transition points so you can be calm, regulated, and true to yourself. Live true to your values.

10. Have fun in the process. Don't forget to laugh, play, and wonder, for in those moments, your greatest insights may surface. You may also find your staff more willing to follow you and, as a result, you will hopefully enjoy the process more.

CHAPTER 4

Looking Out for the Pebble in Your Shoe

Pay attention to the small things

At this point in your leadership journey, you may feel as though you've got some of the big things covered. You may think that this leadership thing isn't that daunting after all. About this time, you realize that it is often the little things that cause you distress. Think about those walks or hikes that you take, and you need to stop because there is a small pebble in your shoe. The pebble must go, or you can't continue your journey. Once removed, you can start again. Some of the things we encounter as leaders feel as though they are big things when they are actually pebbles in our shoe. Let's look at some of the common pebbles.

Step into the importance of communication

Communication can be a small pebble that can turn into a boulder. The nuances of communication may impede your ability to lead your staff during change, growth, or even during business as usual. This is an example of when a small thing can become a big thing.

Sometimes we can miss clues built into body language, tone, intensity, or gesturing. The body can't lie and is the most accurate communication tool we possess. As stated before, a key response here is to listen equally to what is not said as what is said. Listen to the empty space; sometimes answers can be found there. We can also look for dissonance—when someone says one thing and their body seems to say something else. In response to the dissonance, we can say, "I made an observation; would you like for me to share it?" Invariably, the response is affirmative. Then I can share what I observed, without judgment; rather, just with curiosity about what their response or behavior might mean.

For example, I might say, "I notice when you talk about your interactions with a particular client (or colleague), you seem to become tense. Tell me what that is about." Do you see how that can provide an opportunity for the staff member to respond or to unpack what might be going on? They may not even be aware of what they are feeling, and you provided the time and space for them to reflect, in a safe environment. And you asked their permission to share your observation which sets the stage for safety and trust. Most of the time the staff member is grateful for the insight and is willing to examine and potentially identify where their response originates from. This is where their growth can happen.

These are the moments that I truly appreciate. I am always grateful to be a part of the process where staff members can connect dots and increase their self-awareness. I don't take this responsibility lightly and work diligently to approach these times with humility, kindness, and grace with the knowledge that I could be wrong in my observation.

Sowing is a concept presented clearly throughout the New Testament. II Corinthians 9:6 says, "Whoever sows sparingly will also reap sparingly, and whoever sows generously will also reap generously." Sow into others with generous doses of your time, attention, resources, and energy. No one ever provided this for me, and I feel compelled to do this for others as much as it is within my power to do. In the process, you can build relationships that remain even when you aren't working with each other any longer. I am blessed with many of those that I coached, mentored, developed, and encouraged.

Step into being present

An important part of communication is the ability to be present. In this current work environment, pressure to multi-task is incredibly high. We tell ourselves that we can listen while doing a multitude of other things. The reality is that the brain doesn't switch gears as efficiently as we think it does. Our team members deserve our full attention; our ability to listen and give them what they need. This is a discipline that we can develop. It takes practice.

Another element of being present is to listen without thinking of how you will respond. Stay in the moment and just listen. This is something I continue to work on. When I am thinking ahead, trying to create a clever and informed response, sometimes I miss the content or nuance of what is being said.

Another challenge for me is to listen without interrupting. My brain fires quickly and I trick myself into believing that I know where others are going with their thoughts and words, so I often jump in to validate or confirm what they are saying. This is not a helpful leadership practice and is one that I consistently work on. When I am feeling somewhat insecure or dismissed, I may work hard to be heard or to show my significance. Again, this is not a good leadership behavior as it is based in my insecurities. This is also an opportunity to apologize when you find yourself interrupting.

You can demonstrate your humility through an apology.

My hope is that you are ahead of me in your journey and already understand the negative impact of interrupting and you work to avoid it. It is humbling when I find myself, like Paul, doing the very thing I don't want to do. Paul talks about this in Romans 7:19 when he says, "For what I do is not the good I want to do." And can I ever relate to those words! I am a work in progress and will continue to work on this skill and now can catch myself mid-stream when I interrupt. My goal is to prevent my interruptions altogether. My awareness will hopefully help me change my behavior, and I know that change takes time. I am working to be very intentional about this. I consistently pray that the Lord will prompt me to stay attuned to others so that I won't interrupt them.

Step into managing offenses

An additional pebble could be because of offenses created through staff interactions. Maybe you trusted someone and they betrayed your trust. You might feel offended and may even be angry. In your emotional dysregulation, you may even respond in a way that creates additional offenses. I certainly experienced times when I felt betrayed or offended. Those experiences influenced me, causing a reluctance to trust others. This didn't last forever, just for a season, until I was engaged in enough harmonic and authentic relationships to counterbalance the others. And when we are offended or hurt, we can respond emotionally and say or do things that don't align with our values and with how we want to show up.

It is important to me to work from a place of integrity and to honor and respect those that I work with. I don't like situations where I need to be guarded because of lack of trust. For me, that takes a lot of energy that I didn't want to expend or squander. Energy is an important resource, and one that we need to be prudent in how we invest. Not only did I work on this in my personal life, I also ended a couple of my personal friendships because of some betrayals. Only when I became free from the tangled web of these relationships was I able to see the toxicity that was at the basis of my friendships. My friends wanted things on their terms and I worked to appease them, not being my true and authentic self. This was not a healthy spot for me to be in. I didn't realize the negative impacts these friendships held over me.

I am much more cautious now about who I let into that inner circle. Those that are in my inner circle are those that I trust implicitly and love as unconditionally as I can. While it is easy to let people in, it is important that we only let those in that are trustworthy and will build us up. That circle will be small and will take longer than you think it should to develop. It will be worth the investment and time you put into those relationships. I am blessed with women who lead, who love, who laugh, and who learn with me. We often come together over food as a place to nurture our bodies, hearts, souls, and minds. I adore these women and trust them with all of me—not an easy thing to do. And the feeling is mutual as they give me their trust.

Step into the art of forgiveness

As part of moving out of toxic relationships, embracing forgiveness might be part of what is required of you. For me, I know that I need forgiveness when I experience a negative emotional response when I think of a certain event or person. The opposite of that is when I forgive, I no longer experience that rush of emotions when I consider what happened. This can happen when I am ready to respond with grace.

For me, I can extend grace by believing in an alternative explanation for their responses or choices. It is also a way to find a third alternative and remove the blame or hurt that occurs in relationships. This is an example of Romans 12:18 where the scriptures say, "If it is possible, as far as it depends on you, live at peace with everyone." This is something that sets us apart from the unbelieving world. We are taught to live at peace—resolve the conflicts, choose forgiveness, and promote harmony—in your relationships both at work and in your personal life. Harmony doesn't mean that we shy away from difficult conversations; it means that we engage in those conversations with a commitment to grace.

Are there any relationships that you need to come to a closure? Write down here your plan to address these relationships, date them and set an accountability partner.

_____

_____

_____

_____

Even if the difficult conversations end with a staff member leaving, I would like to preserve the relationship. It is important to me that things are left on good terms and not awkward. You know the feeling; you engage in a difficult conversation and then you want to avoid the person at all costs. The awkwardness seems overbearing. When these situations are handled with grace, empathy, and poise, the relationship can be preserved. You can even acknowledge the awkwardness so that you don't let it fester and become toxic or negative. This doesn't mean that we are friends who hang out, it means that if we run into each other at an event, we are not too uncomfortable.

Another element of forgiveness is that you will make mistakes as you travel along. Are you comfortable with asking for forgiveness? What would prevent you from apologizing? A sincere apology is a necessary part of effective leadership. An authentic apology goes a long way in restoring relationships. A good apology should not include defensiveness; it should not try to explain or justify your actions. It is an opportunity to take responsibility for our actions and to admit where we erred.

Yet another layer of forgiveness includes forgiving yourself. Sometimes that is the hardest part of the equation, yet it is necessary if we are to be current in our relationships. Forgiveness also releases us from the tension that unforgiveness creates.

Here are 5 ways you can step into forgiveness:

1. Identify your hurts—who you hurt and who hurt you. Think about how those hurts landed with you and even where they reside in your body, mind, or soul.

2. Ask for forgiveness from others as God leads you.
3. Ask God for His forgiveness.
4. Forgive yourself. This might consist of many steps and may take a while before you are able to fully forgive yourself.
5. Perhaps create a ritual that will help you forgive, such as journaling, writing a letter, or burning the offenses.

Step into the importance of confidentiality

One of the important ingredients that will help your relationships to be preserved is confidentiality. It is vital that you don't talk about staff's issues, performance, or other personal details. Violating this will break trust and may make it difficult to rebuild. When others witness the broken trust, they may react emotionally or be less willing to trust as well. The ramifications of eroding trust are significant and yet can be prevented. This is a simple thing though it's not easy. Brené Brown describes this quality as a vault-that you don't let things out that aren't yours to release. I like the picture of a vault because things don't get out unless you purposefully unlock and open the vault.

Scripture talks about this in Proverbs 10:19 (New American Standard) where it reads, "When there are many words, transgression is unavoidable, but he who restrains his lips is wise." This isn't specific to gossip, and it seems to be very appropriate. It is so tempting when we know something, particularly something juicy, to share with others. And the damage spreads like a wildfire. It is better to show restraint, to prevent the spread of confidential information. When we show that we can maintain confidentiality, we build trustworthiness.

Debi Grebenik, Ph.D.

Step away from jealousy

Another pebble shows up as jealousy or lack of contentment. My husband consistently says that it is unfair to compare. I couldn't agree more, yet we find ourselves looking at others—their positions, their titles, their skills, their reputations, or any number of things. Contentment comes with becoming who God created us to be. Throughout my career, I spent considerable time wishing I were more like others. It took a while to find my own zone. I tried hard to be what I thought everyone else wanted me to be. As you can well imagine, I was frustrated and very ineffective. It doesn't work very well to spend all your time trying to please others. It is counter-productive because we can't please everyone, and sometimes we won't even please anyone. It's beneficial to admire others and want to emulate them. The danger comes in trying to be something you're not. If you focus on that, you will lose your way and become so diluted that you won't even recognize yourself.

It is easy to spend a lot of time chasing the image of who you think you should be. This is a fruitless endeavor. You can spend your time chasing images or you can spend your time cultivating. You can cultivate who you are, your strengths, your vision, and your skills. Becoming the best version of yourself is a much better goal than seeking to conform to what others want for you. Your organization needs your uniqueness, what you bring to your relationships, and your authentic humanness. Step into this—own your journey, with all its imperfections, potholes, and pebbles in your shoes.

I believe that when we seek to be ourselves that God can whisper into our hearts and minds His words of wisdom. When we show up as our authentic selves, we can let others see us and the beauty of our imperfections. We weren't created to only experience the pleasant part of life. We need to embrace the painful part too because that is what will lead to peace and purpose.

Step into pleasing God, not people

Remember, we weren't created to be people pleasers. Our focus needs to be on pleasing God. Pleasing God takes hard work and determination. If we were runners, we wouldn't want to run with a backpack on. The backpack is symbolic of all the expectations we carry around—the things we think we should be doing or how we should be showing up. We can't really compete if we keep that heavy backpack on. What would it take to release it? To cast it off? Hebrews says:

> Therefore, since we are surrounded by such a great cloud of witnesses, let us throw off everything that hinders and the sin that so easily entangles, and let us run with perseverance the race marked out for us (Hebrews 12:1).

This verse doesn't tell us what to be aware of. Rather, it tells us to throw off those things that keep us from moving forward. We are to run with perseverance the race set out for us—the one that will take us to the place that God designed us to be in. Be aware of the things that cling to you. While they may seem appealing, they will derail you. What are some of the things that might be included in this category? Your need for approval, for acceptance, for achievement? Will those hinder you? I know that I don't want to allow things to detour my journey. This is where daily time in God's word allows Him to speak to you through His word. Your friends may also give you feedback when you are veering off-track. Then you can stay the course set before you.

Take a moment to write what you might need to throw off, what is weighing you down, what is making your journey difficult:

_____

_____

_____

_____

As we are running our race, we need to manage our goals. Perhaps the goal needs to shift from being the fastest to finishing. There is something to be said for follow-through, for focus, for finishing. In Hebrews 12:3, "…so that you will not grow weary and lose heart" gives us an important concept to keep us in the race. The word for weary here is an illustration of a runner after they cross the finish line and collapse from exhaustion. Even if we are tired, get up. His strength will become ours. The other thing to consider is if we are making it harder than we should. Are we running with weights? What would it take to release them, to let go? Maybe you developed a blister from this pebble in your shoe. Embrace the pain. Trust the process and look for opportunities for healing.

You may also need to build in some type of maintenance plan where you are checking your gauges. Are you filling yourself with the requirements so that you can finish the race? Are you packing band aids for your blisters? Are you taking a moment to stop so you can remove the pebbles in your shoes? You will get pebbles as they are inevitable. Some are bigger than others. You might be able to continue with some of the smaller pebbles while the bigger ones will completely stop you.

Steps to address the pebbles in our shoes

Embrace being in the valley; trust God's plan for your leadership journey even when you can't see where He is leading you. The valley helps you to appreciate the mountain tops. Sometimes all we can is to embrace the suck—that season we can't control or maybe even see it coming.

When you find pebbles in your shoe, get up; don't give up. You may need to pause so you can remove the pebbles. Embrace the pause, yet don't stay there, keep moving and keep trying.

Sometimes we need to stop so we can shed the things that slow us down. Think about what is in the backpack you are carrying around. What are the things weighing you down? Do you want to remove them and where will you put them? It's important to identify where to unload—find a safe place to leave those things that are causing you to stumble. I Corinthians 9:24 tells us to run in such a way as to get the prize. We can't run to get a prize if we are carrying those things that weigh us down.

It is important to finish. Be aware of the things that will derail or detour you from your path. Acknowledge them and stay the course. II Timothy 4:7 says "I have fought the good fight, I have finished the race, I have kept the faith." There is great value in finishing the race.

Pause and reflect on how comparison to others can cause you to doubt yourself. When we compare ourselves to others, there will always be someone smarter, more successful, or funnier than we are. When we compare ourselves with others, it can become competitive and that interferes with building authentic relationships.

Be sure that you are aware of how jealousy can easily enter your leadership journey. You can easily become jealous of others' skills, reputations, positions, titles, or even styles. Jealousy erodes our ability to connect and collaborate.

Don't be afraid to engage in difficult conversations. Enter those conversations with kindness, grace, and empathy. If we avoid them, the issues seem to keep circling around. Let's be willing to be uncomfortable for a short amount of time as an investment in our relationships. When we step into those courageous conversations, we demonstrate their value to us.

Forgiveness is a crucial element in working with staff. You may need to forgive others and you may need to ask for forgiveness. You will also need to forgive yourself. Sometimes forgiveness is a process, not a one-time event.

Realize the importance of relationships that support, encourage, and challenge you. Lean into those relationships; savor them for what they bring to your life. Make sure they are people where you feel safe. And be sure to be that safe person for others.

Be sure to reflect as you go; regular check-ups are beneficial and help to prevent significant errors and help you to not miss important things. This is another area where you can ask God for His wisdom and for Him to reveal Himself to you. If we ask Him for wisdom, He tells us that He will give it.

CHAPTER 5

Who is walking with you?

Step into walking with others

Before we can invite others to walk with us, we need to know our purpose, why we are here on earth. Philippians 3:12 tells us that there is a specific, unique purpose in life that God designed for you. We can earnestly ask Him to reveal what our purpose is. How do we find this? Think of the time you did something and felt like you were in a zone, or even that time when you got very specific and positive feedback. This also happens when someone you admire, trust, and respect speaks truth into you. My grandmother was that person.

During my college years, I suffered a heartbreak and felt very disheartened because I was trying to follow God's plan for my life. My grandmother, a woman of faith, said to me that she thought God designed a special plan for me and that she thought I would marry a minister. Wow, this was news to me. I thought I knew best and knew who my husband would be. A random visit with a high school teacher ended with her encouraging me to go to seminary after I graduated from college. I prayed about that and felt God's calling in my life and began trying to figure out how to serve God. After some time in prayer, I felt peace about going to seminary.

You guessed it, my first week in seminary I met Mike, and eight months later we were married. My grandparents were at the wedding. My special grandmother spoke truth into me. God used her to give me hope and to dispel my fear. She saw my temporary heartbreak as a step in the journey God planned for me and she was a witness to how God worked in my life and how He provided His best for me. Coincidence it wasn't; divine purpose it was.

That, my friends, is stepping into your purpose. I wish my grandmother was able to see my husband and me serve God in ministry. Unfortunately, six weeks after my wedding, my grandparents were both killed in a car accident by a drunk driver. My grief was overwhelming, yet I knew that my grandmother's legacy would be the hope and purpose she gave me. I wear her wedding ring almost daily because of my dear sweet love for her. My daughter is named after her, further imprinting the legacy she left on my life. Who can you speak into? Who can speak into you? We need to hear and to say the things that breathe life and hope into us. How can you show up in a way that encourages and supports other?

Step into the role of encouraging

Maybe you can encourage and speak into others' lives. Maybe others are speaking into yours. Are you listening? Are you sharing what you observe with those around you? Position yourself so that you can hear from others or so that you can share. The challenge is to wait until others invite you in. Don't just offer your ideas, or you could sound arrogant and as though you know all the answers.

I work with a woman who struggles to see how amazing she is. Periodically, I ask her if I can share what I see. At those moments,

I communicate very specific incidents where she demonstrates a particular attribute. Additionally, I am intentional with helping her step into her gifting. Sometimes, out of fear, we can't see what we bring. This is where we can admonish or encourage others to trust God's word when He says:

> Be gracious to me, O God, be gracious and merciful to me. For my soul finds shelter and safety in you. And in the shadow of Your wings, I will take refuge and be confidently secure until destruction passes by. I will cry to God Most High, who accomplishes all things on my behalf [for He completes my purpose in His plan]. Psalm 57:1-3

How beautiful it is to trust God in His plan to fulfill His purpose in our lives.

Not only can others help us discern His purpose in our lives, God's word can also direct us to His plan and purpose for us. It could be a son, a sermon or through service that we find His purpose because nothing is greater than working from a place of purpose. It took me a while to figure this out; I thought I needed to try and be all things to all people and ended up pleasing no one. This also took a lot of energy trying to do things I wasn't created to do. I am learning to stay in my lane, to embrace God's design for me, and to include other people that will complement my gifting.

As part of your discovery process, you can take assessments to help you find your strengths and areas for improvement. You can also take assessments to find your spiritual gifts. It is important to develop your self-awareness in your giftings and areas that you need to work on. You can also ask others for feedback. Be aware of some people's reluctance to share what they see unless they feel safe with you and trust you. When they embrace the relationship with you, you can solicit their input. Be aware that you may disagree, and in response, try to come from a place of curiosity, not judgment by not defending your perspective. Ask questions by saying "I wonder; tell me more; how does that work?" These responses will build trust, not skepticism, creating the opportunity to engage in authentic conversations based on true observations and insights. And then trust the process, which may take some time for you to build your understanding of who you are and where you want to be. Building our identity takes time and intentional effort to discover and develop.

Step into friendships

We are hard-wired for connection and need relationships. Let's start with a relationship with God. "But they who seek the Lord will not lack any good thing"(Psalm 34:11). When we build a relationship with Him first, that sets the stage for us to create relationships with others. We need relationships as much as we need the air we breathe. They are vital to our survival.

What we don't talk about is how difficult it can be to find friends, to build friendships, and to sustain them. My friendships are my strength and my source of support. They are a result of investment, intention, initiation, and intuition. The investment requires time, emotional energy, and vulnerability. We must be willing to invest in others even knowing that they may not respond in a way we want. There were women that I thought I was connecting with and yet they didn't reciprocate, I was the only one initiating the connections. Those are not the relationships that I pursued or nurtured because they took too much energy rather than giving me energy.

We show our priorities by how we spend our time. We all possess the same amount of time, yet we can choose how to spend it. Because relationships are so important to me, I am willing to invest in certain relationships that will build my friendships. I needed to give up the expectation that others would reciprocate in the way that I wanted. As I accepted this, I was able to enter relationships authentically. These friends can meet me where I am.

Previously, some of my friendships were a little toxic. I didn't always know it at the time and sometimes only realized it after the fact. The friendships were controlling or were very one-sided. At times I felt lonely when friends were few. Now, with intention, I am investing in other women as we build friendships together. They may not know or understand what I do professionally; however, that doesn't keep us from connecting over our humanness, our mistakes, our victories, our sorrows, or our growth. These are the people you celebrate with, run to, or laugh with. These are the women who send you a card for no reason, who text you to say they are thinking of you, or they hold your hand when you are in pain. These are relationships worth their weight in gold and worth your investment.

Intention means an aim or plan. With intention, I made friendships a priority. Maybe you find yourself without these friendships. Psalm 25:16 says "Turn to me and be gracious to me, for I am alone and afflicted. The troubles of my heart are multiplied; bring me out of my distresses." God will give us the desires of our heart when we trust Him in the process.

After finding myself without the friends I craved and needed,

Just Show Up

I chose the word 'connect' as my word for the year a few years ago. With setting my intention for connection, I began reaching out to others—for hikes, coffee, lunch, and various other ways to connect. Interestingly, no one turned me down. I loved learning more about others.

From that intention, several friendships began to emerge. I developed friends to play with, pray with, or pause with. I leaned into their differences and what they could bring to my life. I love the fact that they come with a variety of interests, insights, and intellects. They expand me. They encourage me. And at times, they endure me. I love adventure and novelty, which leads to my love of exploration. Some friends join me in seeking adventure, some are my discussion and thought partners, some are cooking and workout buddies, and some are my advisors. I need them all. Don't be afraid—jump in and risk. Find the women who will lift you up. Set your intention.

Initiating connection requires risk and vulnerability, and the benefits are well worth the effort. Be aware that when you initiate, you may experience some rejection. That is part of the process. The reality is that it is truly lonely at the top. Being a leader can be very isolating, so build your team of supports. You will need them.

Persistence is also valuable as you reach out to others more than once. You might need to attempt to make connections multiple times. Don't let fear keep you from connecting. I still get turned down when I invite others to connect, yet, I won't let that stop me from trying. I hope that you will be vulnerable and reach out to someone. At the very least, you will send them the message that you are interested in them. That's always a good message to send and to receive.

To be kind is more important than being right. Many times, what people need is not a brilliant mind that speaks, they need a gentle heart that listens. And we're back at focusing on how we show up.

Here are 5 ways you can connect with others:

1. Reach out to others, be vulnerable and seek connections.
2. Engage in activities to build. Get out of your comfort zone; try new things. Put yourself in novel situations.
3. Risk rejection and lean into relationships. Put your fear aside and be vulnerable; that's how you will find connection.
4. Make relationships a priority. Try to avoid using the phrase that you're busy; that shuts down the opportunities for connection.
5. Know yourself so you can enter into relationships authentically. Avoid trying to be what you think others want you to be and lean into being who you are.

Step into intuition

Intuition plays a role in how to choose the people to let into your inner circle. These "circlers" (my coined word) need to be intuitive. Sometimes we can't ask for what we need, so it's helpful if our circlers can intuitively meet our needs. For example, not long ago I found myself unmotivated and working from a place of brain fog. I couldn't figure out what was going on and I knew that I wasn't okay. A trusted friend mentioned that she thought I was experiencing grief from my dad's death. It's so easy to miss the signs for ourselves. We need someone we trust to make observations, to lovingly encourage or challenge us. I am so grateful for this friend who put words to my distress. She was correct, and once I realized that I was deep in a grief cloud, I was able to express my emotions, be sad, and the God of all comfort met me in my loss. Make sure you are connected with these people and that you are this type of friend.

Be cautious that you don't move into trying to fix others. You will know you are trying to fix if you find yourself giving advice. We can show up with curiosity and wonder, without judgment. These authentic, trusting relationships are worth nurturing and building. Let's face it, no one really wants someone trying to fix them.

Step into contentment

When we compare ourselves with others, we leave the land of contentment. Paul states in Philippians 4:11 that he learned to be content, regardless of his circumstances. This is an important mindset for us to cultivate. Being content takes practice. It is easy to want more possessions, power, or prestige that what we currently are experiencing.

Contentment is created by finding a state of happiness and satisfaction. Notice the emphasis on the active part of the definition which is *to find*. We can seek contentment with intention. What we put our intention toward becomes our focus. Contentment can be seen in many areas of our lives: with our physical appearance, our homes, our jobs, our relationships, our status, our children, or grandchildren, and many other areas. You can see that the list is long where discontentment can sneak or even barge in.

Be on guard. Discontentment is subtle in its approach, seeding small thoughts or feelings about lack. Pray for a mindset that Paul teaches us about. The result of this type of contentment is that we will be ready because it is Christ in us that will give us the inner strength, confidence, and peace that we need. And God will certainly strengthen us to do what He calls us to do. This is what we call 'working in your zone.' Spend most of your time there even though we all still need to do things that we don't particularly like or are called to do because our jobs require those tasks of us. Paul admonishes us in Philippians 4:11 to be content in any and every situation because we trust in Christ.

Step into lifting up

One other thing that is a sign of an effective leader is how we lift others up. To *lift* means to raise to a higher level or position. Let's use that as our working definition. How can we help others rise to different levels? What levels might we aspire to? How about a level where others become all they were created to be? What if we encourage others to see themselves as we see them, as God sees them? What if we love them, even when it's difficult? What if we give them acceptance? Those are all indicators of lifting others up and developing them. Who lifted you up? How did they do it and how meaningful was it to you?

When we lift others, we are positioning them higher because they are worthy of it. This is a great way to show up in humility by letting people shine without feeling threatened. Lifting can also include sending a note of encouragement, a gift, or a text to let another person know you are thinking of them or that you've got their back. When we are seen and heard, we can know that we are valued. To *appreciate* means to increase the value of. When we express appreciation and gratitude, we increase another's value. I still cherish hand-written notes. I love to write them and to receive them. I love when I see notes I wrote placed on others' bulletin boards or desks. Words create legacies and are powerful to build or raise up others. What kind of legacy do you want? To build confidence, esteem, and hope or to destroy purpose?

Identify a few ways that you can lift others up now:

_____

_____

_____

_____

Step into changing your language

It's worth taking a moment to revisit the power of words. One of the things I try to do is to avoid value-laden words. This is difficult, yet once you begin doing this, you can't go back. Pay attention to words that could sound judgmental such as *should* or *must*. We don't want to shame or blame others—we want to encourage and build up. I needed to work on this—a lot! What other words might imply judgment or shame? I also try to avoid saying 'trigger' because that is associated with a gun. I choose to use 'activate' instead. What if we avoid words such as manipulate, crazy, and defiant?

What other words would you like to avoid or replace?

_____

_____

_____

_____

I believed that since one of my spiritual gifts is prophecy, it was my duty and responsibility to tell others what to do and how to do it. You can imagine how well that was received (it wasn't) and I lost some friends over my desire 'to help.' When the Holy Spirit began gentling my approach and gifting, I was able to use my gifts to guide others to see their own gifts, talents, and strengths. I was learning how to lift others up with my words without judging or shaming them. This is progress! Thank you, Lord, for working on me to become a guiding rather than a judging light. I must be sure to manage my own wellbeing so I can continue to respond from a place of love and grace rather than from stress and frustration. One of the best responses leaders can provide is to prioritize how

Just Show Up

they show up, so that they lead with kindness and generosity of spirit. Giving grace is important.

As you spend much of your time and energy on lifting others, you may find that it can be lonely at the top. Sometimes you may be so focused on the journey of getting from A to B that you don't realize you are out on the limb by yourself. People may not follow closely or at the same pace. That's a normal response. Therefore, it is vital to include those in your circle so when you feel alone, you can tap into those people you trust and respect. You will be able to ask for what you need. That helps us to stay in the game even when it's difficult. We all need support in our journey. You can't be the one that only gives—you need to be able to receive as well. This is where you can tap into and see the value that relationships bring to your life.

Step into living from intention

To be regulated in your relationships, tap into intention. Set your intentions to reflect, reset, and rejuvenate. What prevents you from doing this? Is it a sense of urgency, that you can't stop, wondering what others are thinking about you, or is it your own fear and anxiety? Is your work your sense of identity?

This Photo by Unknown Author is licensed under CC BY-ND

There is a Japanese concept called *wabi-sabi* that means imperfect beauty and it prizes authenticity. The building blocks of wabi-sabi are: Nothing lasts forever.

Nothing is ever finished. Nothing is truly perfect. How can you incorporate this into your life? How can you embrace imperfections? Who will you invite into this journey with you? If you can truly embrace a wabi-sabi approach, you can stop striving for perfection and, instead, focus on God's perfect plan for you.

This shift of perspective celebrates our flaws and sees those flaws as assets. Isn't that how God sees us? I Corinthians 1:27 tells us that God chose the foolish things of the world, the weak things, and the lowly things. I'm so grateful that He chose me. Now I want to rest in Him. Sometimes I need to slow down enough to see what God plans for me and then to reflect on what He's taught me as part of the process.

Sometimes we get stuck only seeing things one way. Here is a logo that we all see regularly.

When you look at it, you may only see the image at the top. Look again and notice the arrow in the logo. Did you see that before? Sometimes we only see things as they first appear. Look again, look beyond the surface. Now that you've seen the arrow, you won't be able to unsee it. Look for the less obvious in your work and your daily world. Savor the moments. Pay attention and be observant.

One way to reflect and reset might be through journaling, experiential activities, or an individual or group retreat. Set apart time for just you. You are worth it, and you need it. Sometimes reflection can happen with others, and sometimes it is best on your own. One year, I met with a friend in January to review our previous year and set intentions for the new year. We also both chose a word for the new year. It was incredible to spend that time thinking, reminiscing, and planning. It was fun to do that with a trusted friend because we were both able to gain keen insights and use those in planning for the upcoming year. Perhaps you can create something similar as an ending and beginning.

A concept I recently learned was to quit using the conjunction *but*, substituting it with *and* instead. I can reflect individually *and* collectively; I can be sad *and* excited; and I can be afraid *and* brave. We can hold two places without their being mutually exclusive. What polarities might you be engaging in? When we are stressed or come from a trauma history, we tend to gravitate toward black-and-white thinking. These polarities can become extreme. Be aware of your tendency to go there.

What are some of the polarities you are engaging in?

_____

_____

_____

_____

Step into learning to discharge

Somewhere along the way, we often receive the message that a stiff upper lip is the way to go or that you just need to tough it out. Let's look at the opposite of that. What would happen if you let out your frustrations? What are the advantages of discharge? You will reap physical, emotional, intellectual, and spiritual benefits.

Think of David who cried out to God throughout the book of Psalms. My paraphrase is that he was saying "Really, God? Why? And why me?" You might feel something similar at times. Can you find ways to discharge through running, talking, painting, singing, dancing, riding, or even drumming? What we don't let out gets stored in our bodies and can create a sense of being stuck or rigid. The stress hormone, cortisol, stays in the body for 30 days unless discharged. With chronic stress, cortisol's impact can become significant. Think of the release you felt after a good cry; the body needs flow to function effectively.

I am a verbal processor and find discharge in talking through something. And now, the older I get, the more benefit I realize from time spent walking or running by myself where I can think or zone out. We all need different ways to discharge. I also find great release in laughter and play. There's nothing like playing a game or baking with one of my grandchildren. We are silly and playful, creating an opportunity to let go of those emotions that are causing me distress. Engaging in these experiences also require that I am fully present with them in the moment. These opportunities for discharge keep us living in the present without focusing on the past or worrying about the future.

Step into helping others see over the wall

Our job as leaders is to think what, not how. We can show up with imagination without knowing all the answers. For example, an African impala can jump ten feet high and thirty feet long yet will be trapped behind a four-foot wall if they can't see over it. That's a good metaphor for leadership. We need to help others see over the wall so that they can move and go where they want and maybe jump over their own walls. Our job may be to lift them up enough to see what was blocking their views. Or we may find ourselves helping others to tear down the barricades in their way so they become unstuck. This is exciting work as others clear their way and find their path. Or we may be the cheerleader cheering them on as they attempt to jump over the wall.

Steps to finding your purpose

1. Find your purpose by seeking God and listening to others' input about your life and calling. Pause and listen; read God's word and ask Him to speak to you. Let Him speak to you through books, songs, podcasts, or friends that you trust.

2. Build a circle of friends and be diligent to build this in your life. Risk rejection to find connection.

3. Create authenticity in your relationships. Share your vulnerability so you can connect with others.

4. Speak into others' lives; develop, encourage, and grow with them. This is the beauty of leadership.

5. Set intentions—for connection, for fun, for learning, or for whatever it is that you value or want to expand. Pray for discernment about what to set your mind on. Setting an intention is not saying 'I want wealth' and believing it will happen. Rather, setting an intention is focusing on God and asking Him to show us His plan. Then we can follow up in the way He directs. An intention is where we put our energy and resources. Be wise

about how you spend yours.

6. Initiate connections and be vulnerable. Be persistent. You may need to ask others more than once. Be creative in building your friendships. Find different types of people and engage in various activities with them.

7. Use your intuition to discover what others need from you as you build relationships with them.

8. Lift others up. Look for ways to encourage others through kindness, gratitude, and generosity. Give freely of your time, energy, and resources.

9. Take time to regulate yourself. Perhaps you can find balance through taking time to reflect and relate. We can show up for others when we are calm and regulated. When we are distressed, it's harder for us to be there for those or what we care about. For me, working out daily is one way to manage my stress and keeps me regulated. I do this first thing in the mornings and I know that is not what will work for everyone. Find what works for you and then commit to it.

10. Find ways to discharge. Remember, what we don't release stays in our body, often resulting in headaches, stomachaches, high blood pressure, weight gain or loss, or a multitude of other maladies. Discharge options are varied and need to include what will work for you. Do you need to walk it out? Run it out? Cry it out? Talk it out? Throw or punch it out? The key is to find ways to get it out of your body. Sometimes words aren't enough, so movement might be what you need.

CHAPTER 6

Building Your Power Walkers

Step into walking

Walking with someone makes the journey so much better. This is true in almost all areas of our lives. The beauty of leadership is cultivating relationships with those you are supervising. It takes time, energy, and resources, and the investment is well worth it. I find this to be the fun part of leadership.

Let me tell you about one of those fun experiences. Let's call her Melissa (as you guessed, this is not her real name). I worked with Melissa previously and knew of her work ethic and how good she was with people. So, I swooped in and recruited her to come work at the organization I was leading. I brought her in as one of the organizational leaders in a totally new position. During her first year in this position, she and I logged many hours together trying to build her position. While she is incredibly smart, she found herself in a new role and a new skill set. Many times, the conversation in my office centered around how inept she felt. We must attend to others' emotional content as well as their skills or tasks they engage in.

We can't be afraid to lean in and talk about vulnerable topics. She often asked me why I hired her and if I were sure she was the person for the position. We spent a lot of time unpacking her personal insecurities, fears, anxieties, and questions. I tried hard to create a safe space where she didn't feel judged or shamed. As we processed, she gained insights and courage about her role. It was fun to watch her blossom. She now laughs about how little she knew when she started. Yet, I continued to remind her of how I believed in her and could see her potential. I tried hard to not exaggerate, to just build on her strengths in an honest and genuine way.

You may be wondering what I mean when referencing a safe space. Several things contribute to making a safe space where you can feel secure. Be trustworthy by doing what you say you will do when you say you will do it. Be transparent, honest, and authentic. Other components that build safety include not judging, shaming, or blaming. This can be difficult to create. We need to allow others to be vulnerable, to not know, to express doubts and anxieties all without fear of being criticized. When we feel free to be who we are, we can use our energy to create and to be our best selves. I think this is God's design for all of us and yet it is very difficult to craft in most situations.

Only after you establish a safe place can you begin to build trust. Trust is the foundation of relationships, both personal and professional. Trust develops with consistency over time. Mean what you say, do what you say, and follow through on what you say. It takes time to build trust and only moments to erode it. Be careful. Ephesians 4:29 says to "Let no unwholesome word come out of your mouths, but only what is helpful for building others up…"

During the first year, Melissa focused on learning the content of the position. The second year, as her understanding grew, she began to step into her leadership role with confidence and competence. We continued spending time together, talking about what she was doing as well as how to do it. By the third year, she was at a mastery level, with people all over the state consulting her expertise. She began to develop others and was well-respected. Her insights were evident, and she helped to direct the organization toward excellence. Her sense of competence helped her to create and innovate solutions to programmatic challenges. I gave her the gift of time—my time and her time to grow and develop; both were needed.

She and I continued to meet consistently, discussing her personal and professional growth. She continues to evolve as a leader—one that I respect and admire. She leads with humility and grace, and those she supervises respect her. I can't begin to tell you how blessed I feel to be part of her journey. We are still friends, and I value her opinion. She teaches me, and I appreciate her perspective. She shows up with wisdom, and I now lean into her. You know, this is a true mark of leadership. If you look around you and don't see anyone following or you aren't developing anyone, you may want to question how you are leading.

Step into developing others

As you build your power walkers, those that can stay up with you, you will become the leader God intended you to become. Isn't that exciting? One other thing to think about when developing your power walkers is that some won't possess the grit needed to do the work. It's okay to not invest your time and energy in those people. Be prudent about how you invest your resources. Choose the people who want to develop and that are accepting, nonjudgmental, and teachable. There are many people that will respond to your leadership, so choose wisely. And then go all in.

You know, I struggled at first with the concept of developing others. That still, small voice in my head kept saying, "Who do you think you are? Why would anyone want to listen to you? What do you have to offer?" Instead of letting my doubts or shame rule, I persevered and stepped into this space even with my doubts and questions. You can too. I also realized that the Bible highlighted many leaders with questionable behaviors. Abraham lied about his wife, Moses murdered an Egyptian, David committed adultery and then murder, Solomon turned toward idolatry, and Peter denied Jesus. I think I am in pretty good company because God used these leaders in mighty ways, flaws and all. It isn't really about our perfection; rather, it's more about our availability to His leading and our obedience once He shows us His plan for us. It's not simple and yet God provided a game plan for us.

How do you figure out who to invest in? Look for those who are very teachable. This is the biggest characteristic I look for in hiring and in supervision. Teachability is a mindset—a perspective that they don't know everything, that they want to learn, and usually includes an element of humility. I am confident that we can teach skills as long as they are teachable. This characteristic also seems to create advancement opportunities.

Invest in those who are willing to work at their growth. Are they willing to increase their self-awareness? Will they pursue additional help or supports to enhance their growth? Are they currently investing in their growth through reading, listening to podcasts, or other growth-oriented activities? If they meet most of these criteria, these are your people, these are the ones worthy of your investment. Remember, Jesus only chose twelve to develop, teach, and invest in. And you can step into the role of encouraging, challenging, and guiding with those who are willing to grow. Be judicious about your choices as well.

Step into mistakes

Also look at your staff's relationship with failure, with errors, or with imperfections. Do they embrace their errors? Do they talk about their missteps? This is important as you choose who to develop. Knowing this about them will guide you in your choices of who to invest in. Use this insight in your decision-making.

You also need to be aware of your own relationship with failure and how this affects your decision-making, your vulnerability, and your leadership. If you can view those errors as part of your learning process, you are less likely to feel shame. And then you can be vulnerable and share your mistakes with those you supervise. This will pave the way for others to share their vulnerabilities, and you both will grow because of it. Look at how your staff responds to mistakes. Are they okay with imperfections, or do they think they need to be perfect? If they can look at their missteps as learning opportunities, they are probably teachable.

Did you ever consider that you can create a relationship with your failures? We can ignore our errors, or we can trust them to teach us. Be aware that you may experience significant feelings when you err or fail. Try to trace the origin of those feelings. Perhaps they came from parents who were critical of you or from the voices in your head that say you aren't good enough. Your sense of self-worth may suffer when you make mistakes. How will you combat those feelings? What will be the story you tell yourself?

Try these scripts on:
- "I am human and making mistakes is part of being human."
- "I am doing the best I can."
- "I am doing the best I know to do at this time."
- "Well now I know how not to do this."
- "What can I learn from this mistake?"
- "What is the worst thing that could happen?
- "Will the consequences affect me long-term?"
- "This is part of my learning journey."
- "I can learn from this and do better next time."

What might happen if you shifted the narrative? These scripts can keep you from beating yourself up and from spiraling in shame. You can expect to experience a visceral response to your mistakes. None of us likes to fail; however, you can modulate the amount of impact you let it make on your life. If you find yourself stuck or spiraling in your mistakes, seek out other leaders who will help you shift or gain perspective. Perspective helps us to stay grounded, while a skewed perspective can derail us. Proverbs teaches us that there is safety in the counsel of others. Regularly find those you can consult with-it will be worth the effort.

Steps toward connection

Another important concept to think about is simple and easy to remember: Connect before you correct. This saying is appropriate for all relationships—parent/child, professional supervision, and even marriage. When we focus on the relationship rather than compliance, then and only then will we begin to see results. When we focus on compliance, we may get performance without passion or loyalty. Sometimes the compliance will come out of fear rather than commitment to the mission or purpose of the organization. When we connect first, we build relationship, safety, trust, and understanding.

Here is how this works. Connection means that I ask how those I supervise are doing instead of only addressing task completion or performance concerns. This is not therapy. This is about focusing on human connection. I also acknowledge their contributions and express gratitude for what they bring to the organization. I am letting them know that I see them and see all they are dealing with. It's important that we validate the struggles, stresses, and successes. As we build our relationship and trust with others, they tend to want to be coached and guided in their professional development. Then it becomes fun. It is well worth the wait and the work of building the connection.

This concept is also relevant in your personal relationships. Isn't it more important to be connected than to be right? Yikes, did I really say that? I like being right, having the last word, and letting others know it—*and* that doesn't really build relationships. Thankfully, God intervened so that I quit going down that road of self-absorption. Now I find that I really like leaning in on connection because I see the value of the relationships I create in the supervisory role.

Step into building joy

When you get a handle on building relationships through connection, you can engage in seeking joy. Find what things you can do from your soul. Those things will be different for each person and may not make sense to others. You can also choose joy over regret. Rather than looking backwards over what was or wasn't, you can choose to seek joy—that abiding presence of God in your life. Sometimes we avoid thinking or talking about joy for fear that it will disappear. We are afraid of things being too good. Think of a newborn sweetly sleeping. In fear and anxiety, we may move close to the baby to make sure he or she is breathing. That is called *foreboding joy*. We are so afraid to lean into joy that we freeze up, waiting for something awful to occur rather than spending time basking in pure joy.

Invite others into your joy bubble. We shy away from using words such as joy in the workplace. I think we should conduct joy retreats, joy quotes, and anything you can that will build joy into the lives of those you supervise or work with. It would be so much fun to hear people describe their jobs as being "joyologists" (my term) or joy promoters. We all love being around others who build people up, who find joy. This doesn't mean that you aren't authentic or don't struggle; it means that you are unshakeable in your faith and convictions. It means that your confidence is not found in things, situations, or titles; your sense of self is found in who God created you to be. With that knowledge, you can show up with joy. Now doesn't that sound worthy of our attention, our pursuit? I say yes! Let's create joy bubbles and invite others into them.

What are some joy bubbles you can create? For yourself? For others?

_____

_____

_____

_____

How we describe ourselves to others says something about how we see ourselves. We typically describe ourselves by the roles we hold rather than how we show up. Our roles are what we do yet aren't the entirety of our existence. What if we put more focus on describing ourselves by our kindness, our humility, our vulnerability, and other traits? We can focus on what we do or who we are. When we develop and grow who we are, what we do improves in the process. How we engage in relationships is the most important part of what we do. We are hard-wired for relationship and connection, so we need to make sure that we put our time and energy there. This is the simple truth, yet it's not very easy.

Leadership is leading people. Managing is managing tasks and processes. When we lead people, we need to focus on relationships. This can be the difficult part of leadership, or the easy and fun part. Sometimes we focus on all we need to do and neglect how we do those things. Relationships should include laughing, dreaming, growing, and developing.

When we focus on relationships, we need to manage our risk. Involvement with others creates vulnerability and risk of being hurt, of failing, of letting someone down, of disappointing others, and of becoming overwhelmed. On the flip side of that risk, you might experience delight, wonder, joy, encouragement, growth, and respect. The benefits are well worth the risks.

Show up, all in, without reservation. That is what leadership is all about. Live without regrets of the things you wish you'd done or the person you wish you'd become. Recently I experienced a growth spurt in this area. With a new colleague, I found myself coming across too strong when we were working on a project. Because of the value I place on relationships, I paused and took a moment to apologize. The apology was genuine, and the other person received it with genuine appreciation. Prioritizing connection is an intention we can set and one we can honor with our words, actions, and energy. Be clear about the intentions you set.

Then enjoy the fruits of your investment in relationships. One of the best things about spending time developing and investing in others is when they begin to develop and invest in others, taking the lessons learned into their leadership. This, my friends, is what I live for. I get so excited when others use the lessons from our journey to teach and guide those they lead. They become our work grandchildren. What a legacy we can leave. The legacy can outlive us if we are willing to put in the time and energy. Make no mistake, this takes time and can be very taxing (and delightful, fun, and exciting too).

Here are 5 ways to build your joy:
1. Plan time for those things that fill your bucket.
2. Find others that share your commitment to joy.
3. Build in joy moments (watchin0p5g videos of babies laughing).
4. Show up as your true and authentic self—this gives others room to be their best selves.
5. Nurture your soul—artistically, spiritually, and culturally.

How can you engage in these ways to build joy:

_____

_____

_____

_____

Step into taking chances

Leadership can also gravitate toward the familiar. Be aware that you can change your trajectory. You can shift your perspective at any time. You can focus or refocus on your own growth and skills. You can engage in your own leadership coaching in training, reading books, listening to podcasts, or any way to improve or expand your skills. Look for ways to create micro-changes.

You don't need to think about an overhaul—you can make small choices to create incremental changes. Those micro-changes add up to bigger changes or to tipping points. Think of it as training for a marathon. Your first day of training you don't go out and try to run twenty miles. You start with one or two miles and build from there. That is what building your leadership muscle looks like.

Change can be created in phases:
- Phase 1: Intention—Build awareness
- Phase 2: Intervention—Build integration
- Phase 3: Impact—Build transformation

Start with creating the buzz or awareness about where you are going and about the change that is coming. Then determine how to build the change into existing programming and processes. This is the integration phase. The impact occurs when the transformation begins. As things start to shift and the culture of change is infused, that's when you begin to feel the impact.

Phase 1 is where norms are developed, values, language and philosophy are created. Resources are allocated for upcoming changes. Phase 2 includes paper changes as well as potential staffing changes. Positions and responsibilities may shift to create alignment with the awareness and intention built in phase 1. Phase 3 creates sustainability through staff training, changes in supervision practices and focus. You might revise tools to be in alignment with identified goals. These phases build clear and consistent messaging and transformation strategies.

Remember, change can feel hard and progress may feel slow

and fast all at the same time. This is the time to celebrate the small wins as you experience them.

We shouldn't expect others to do things we aren't willing to do. If we are expecting those we lead to engage in their growth and development, we need to invest in our personal growth and development. This is a significant message to communicate through your actions and attitudes. We want those we lead to be teachable, thus we need to emanate that.

My experience is that once you reach a certain level of leadership, less and less time is spent on our own development because we are too busy taking care of our role's requirements. In my leadership coaching, I often hear from others that they were never taught how to lead, nor do they get supervision about how to handle employee challenges. This is a flaw in our organizations. Development should occur for all positions in organizations. Just because we are in leadership roles does not mean that we don't still need to grow and be challenged. Seek out growth opportunities that will stretch you. Not only does it model that development is valuable and important, but you will also be better for it.

Step into serving

Interestingly, the Bible teaches us that we give to receive and the last shall be first—so the concepts of serving to lead should not come as a surprise. When we approach our leadership as a servant, we can show up with others' needs at the forefront. Serving also suggests that we don't ask others to do anything we aren't willing to also do.

When I was the director of a boys' residential home, I was cooking lunch one day because the cook called out sick. One of the residents came up to me and said, "Mrs. G, why are you doing the cooking?" I responded and said that I didn't believe I should ask anyone to do something I wasn't willing to do. With an incredulous nod, he said that he thought that was cool. That's an example of being a servant. This was an excellent object lesson on what a different style of leadership could look like. In contrast, servant leadership puts the followers' best interests first. This is an opportunity to show a different pathway of leadership.

Step into giving feedback

When we prioritize others' needs and growth, we realize the value of feedback. When asked, most people say they want their feedback directly. Directness can gravitate toward abruptness. This is a difficult process, and when we get nervous, we often say too much. Be wary of this tendency. Brief is better, especially when bolstered by kindness.

When we are willing to take risks and give feedback, we can show up with kindness and integrity, honoring the process. This is the time to give clear expectations because without clarity it is difficult to guide someone to success. Be aware that at times someone may respond defensively, and your challenge at this point is to not respond similarly. Your role is to remember that your feedback is causing stress for your staff member. This is not personal—it may be due to their personal history or experience. Your staff member will read more from your tone, body language, and intensity than they will from your words. Be aware of what you are communicating intentionally and unintentionally.

Sometimes I don't do this very well. What I learned is to watch the person's responses and gauge how what I said landed.

For example, I often thought what I said was calm, leveled, and clear, and yet when I look at a colleague, I can see tension or anxiety in their facial expression or body language. Because of that response, I needed to modify or change my response to ensure they are hearing what it is that I am communicating. It is also incumbent on me to restate the information in a different way so that they may be able to hear it.

This process is worth the effort. You create the opportunity to build someone else up, to increase their skills, to challenge them to new levels, and to create a better organization as a result. Do you want to be the leader than leans in or the one that avoids conversations that might be a little awkward? Did anyone engage in these conversations with you? If not, you might need to ask for specific feedback. This is part of your own development. Be ready to hear things you don't really want to hear, and be ready to stay calm and not defensive when you hear constructive criticism. You can ask for clarification or examples that will guide you as you grow professionally and personally.

Even though I think I am somewhat self-aware, I still find some feedback surprising. Perhaps it is part of my need for competence. It is humbling to be far in your career and others identify things that still need to be worked on. I don't know about you; however, I kind of want to just coast in this phase of my career. And it seems that we can never get to a place of just coasting—we must continue to grow. When we don't focus on growing, we become stale and complacent, and neither of these characteristics lends itself to effective leadership. Remember, you are the only one who will care about your own development. Make your growth a priority. Dedicate your time, energy, and resources to align with your priority of growth. And be sure to engage in fun along the way.

This chapter is all about some of the relational elements of leadership. We can't neglect these components. Attend to this side of leadership as much as, if not more than, the technical skills required in strategic leadership. I like to read books to inspire me and to guide my conversations with others. I also like to talk to others as part of my self-awareness. Remember, it's a journey, not a destination. You won't arrive, you will find detours for the journey, side roads, or maybe even some speedbumps along the way.

Stay the course even when you can't see your way forward. You might need others to light the way for you. While you may take a momentary pause, try to keep moving. Emotions such as fear, anxiety, disappointment, or even frustration may enter in and threaten to cause a freeze response. Be aware that this may occur and set your intention on how you will respond. Be ready, this may take energy that you didn't plan to expend.

Steps to Building Others

1. Be picky about who you choose to work with and develop. The resources of your time and energy are limited, so be prudent about where you invest them. Ask for a commitment from those you see potential in.

2. Develop a relationship with your mistakes. You will make them. Accept that they are part of your journey and can derail you or cause growth surges. Will they define you? Will they be part of your story? How do you interact with your mistakes? What is the story you

are telling yourself about your mistakes? Can you identify the stories others are telling about their mistakes/ How does that impact your work culture?

3. Focus on building connection before you spend time correcting. Create trust and focus on relationship-building before jumping in to give feedback. Connect before you correct. Prioritize the relationship.

4. Avoid focusing on being right; some things are signficantly more important. Identify what is more important to you and concentrate on that.

5. Develop the things that matter—your relational skills. Those will contribute to and improve your leadership skills.

6. Set intentions about what you value. Prioritize those intentions with your energy, expertise, and enthusiasm.

7. Develop others so they can develop others. Don't lead from a place of a scarcity mindset. Lead from a place of generosity and sharing.

8. Know that you can grow and expand your skills at any time. Take steps to improve your skills. Engage in coaching, training, reading, or listening. Understand that you can grow your skills at any phase of your leadership journey.

9. Ask for feedback so that you can grow and develop your own leadership skills. Ask from those you trust, those that can provide helpful, accurate feedback that will contribute to your professional development.

10. Giving feedback requires responding from a calm, regulated perspective. Notice responses and adjust your tone or intensity accordingly. Remind yourself that the benefits are worth the effort required to complete this step.

CHAPTER 7

And now what?

Step into coming full circle

As you build your leadership toolbox, be sure to spend time getting equipped. Equip yourself with what you need to stay the course. What do you need to finish strong? My career spans decades, and I am as excited about the work now as I was at the beginning of my career. I intentionally cultivate this mentality by engaging in ongoing learning, exploring ways to grow, and entering novel experiences. I hope you find your pathway to staying fresh. It is worth the effort.

As part of my personal journey, I learned how important it is to invest in my own self-care. As I made my wellbeing a priority, I was also modeling this for those I supervise. They could see that it was a priority to invest in the practices that will keep you going strong. Burn-out occurs when we deplete our resources of our energy, motivation, and time. We must keep filling our bucket or we will find ourselves without reserves. It is very similar to developing a savings account. You can't spend everything that you make. You need to be prudent and save some of your resources for other times.

I find that small investments early on begin to add up and fill my bucket, which positions me to keep going. Here is what this looks like. As my career progressed, I focused on only taking positions that were flexible so that I could work from a place of my values. For me, one of my top values is family. When my children were growing up, I tried to make their events a priority by putting them on my calendar and working around them. If there were a soccer game on Tuesday at 4:00 p.m., I would go in early that day or work longer the day before. Then I didn't struggle with guilt or shame for not living in alignment with my values. There were times when scheduling didn't quite work out, and I needed to accept that I fell short those days. Now I prioritize being at my grandchildren's events as often as I can to let them see (and hear) my support. And I feel as though I am honoring and living according to my values. This also sets an example of the importance of the relationships I value.

I remember being offered a position in the prison system, and I declined it. They told me that if there were a security issue, they could shut the prison down and I wouldn't be able to leave. I envisioned missing out on birthdays, graduations, and other rites of passage. I declined the offer and am grateful for the other opportunities that came along. While it was significantly more money, the personal cost seemed to be greater than the benefit. I couldn't see myself in a position that could be confining and not allow for any flexibility.

I also applied for multiple positions that were beyond my level of expertise. I only wanted someone to give me a chance. I often told my husband that I was putting my foot in the door and that one of these days the door would open. I risked and put myself out there. By pursuing a variety of opportunities, I felt that I could tap into options. Knowing there are options and choices helps us to feel excited and energized about the work we do. That is another strategy for staying the course. Knowing you can make choices helps you choose to stay the course. And let's face it, it feels pretty good to be wanted, to know that someone sees your value and worth. That process can be part of what contributes to your self-care and sense of fulfillment.

We also need to be willing to advocate for ourselves around working conditions and salary. Using our voice creates contentment and satisfaction when we know that we can ask for what we need and value. Can you negotiate for a salary that supports your education and experience? Be sure to put value on your value. Sometimes in our efforts to be humble we lose sight of confidence. Confidence comes from competence. Competence is the sweet intersection of knowledge and skills. It is not enough to know. You must know what to do with the knowledge. It is this sweet spot where wisdom emerges. God can grant that—He gives us wisdom when we ask for it. I don't know about you, but I am asking daily, -actually moment by moment, for wisdom. I need heavenly wisdom in my leadership journey.

Another strategy I engaged in was to obtain the education, certifications, and training that would position me for what was my heart's desire. For me, teaching is my favorite thing to do. So, I pursued my doctorate—a dream of mine since I was sixteen years old. Important to note is that my family didn't really emphasize education. My mom never graduated from high school, my dad only went to one year of college, and of my three siblings, only one of them went to college and only for one year. So, I am an anomaly in my family, and I tried to step into and own my journey and my heart's desire by positioning myself in the best light that I could. It took commitment of my time, energy, and money, and I wouldn't change a thing about the process. Can you say that? Can you position yourself so that you can look back without regret? I followed my dream and was able to do this because of the unfailing support of my husband and children.

Step into authenticity

Authenticity means being genuine. This is also includes owning our uniqueness, flaws, beauty, and talents. One caveat I want to add to this discussion is while you can embrace being yourself, you may need some assistance on the journey.

What keeps you from being authentic? Take a moment to reflect on those limitations.

_____

_____

_____

_____

Whatever do I mean by that? Many of us experienced trauma in our childhoods or adulthood. Because we didn't talk about trauma prior to the last several years, your history may include experiences that we now identify as traumatic, such as abuse, neglect, bullying, poverty, or many other experiences. The imprint of those experiences can be significant, leaving a trail of anxiety, pain, insecurity, hurt, and other emotional residue. I want to encourage you to go get professional help if trauma is part of your story. You may need someone to work with you to help you heal so that you can show up as your best self and lead others. Doing the healing work will also impact your personal relationships. God can weave together our innermost parts, or your healing may come from an experienced therapist.

Authenticity can occur if, and only if, we do our own work. Be real with yourself first. That's where authenticity begins. It may feel too difficult, yet the process paves the way to authenticity, a worthy goal. And then persevere in your healing and growth. Don't shy away from the hard stuff, lean into it. Step out and be bold. Embrace all of your story as it contributes to and creates who you are and how you will lead.

I love to use the metaphor of a quilt in talking about our authenticity and uniqueness. The different pieces design our own personal quilt. That quilt is what others see. Make sure you stitch it together and don't leave pieces incomplete or frayed. Be bold in your quilt design. Become the best version of your quilt that you can and own it. When we do that, it creates the space for others to be who they are. And that, my friends, is authenticity in action. Don't be afraid to look inside—you might like what you find. And don't be afraid that the underside of the quilt contains frayed edges, loose threads, and maybe some extra stitches. Those imperfections are what creates the beautiful quilt.

As you seek self-awareness and healing, be ready for the long haul. It may be quite a journey. You need to push through even though you might be tempted to bail and quit the process. I know at times I wanted to settle into complacency and not stay the course. I thought I could float on my skills and coast into just being good enough. While that seemed to be an acceptable goal, I knew I wouldn't be content if I settled for mediocrity. So, I decided to push forward and embrace all the parts of myself in the process, even the parts that I didn't really like.

Now I would describe my leadership style as messy and real, less than perfect with lots of mistakes. I decided to embrace courage over comfort and to engage in the messiness that authenticity creates. On the other side of my decision was the journey I was waiting for. I love learning about leadership and growing. Coasting and complacency wasn't an option for me. It seemed appealing yet I knew wasn't a long-term solution for me. So glad I kept going into the unknown, into expanding, and into a lifelong learning adventure.

Here are 5 ways you can be more authentic:

1. Be honest with yourself.
2. Engage in difficult conversations where truth is told.
3. Surround yourself with others who are also committed to authenticity.
4. Embrace your flaws—do what you can to improve and then move to acceptance.
5. Give yourself some self-compassion.

How do you plan to build more authenticity into your life?

_____

_____

_____

_____

Step into consistency

Staff will look at leaders for their consistency. Consistency creates calm, trust, and predictability. When predictability is present, safety occurs. Safety allows us to show up as our authentic selves. Stability in mood is a good place to start. II Timothy 4:5 states "But as for you, be clear-headed in every situation [stay calm and cool and steady] ..." Being clear-headed allows us to lead from a place of consistency and calm. This is where we start—with our mood and demeanor.

Our emotions create contagion, meaning others will catch our mood. You know what I mean. If you show up at the office with a 'tude (short for attitude), others may soon develop their own 'tudes, and pretty soon there are a lot of 'tudes in the office. This may not create the environment you were looking for. Rather, you could show up with a consistency that shows your calm. I know that at times one of my staff would come in my office to just settle into my "chill." Thus, it is important that I manage my emotional content so that I can be that calm person required for the organization I work in.

Consistency creates trust also. What if every day when you showed up to work your desk was in a different place? Would you find that stressful? I sure would. This is how it feels to others when we change policies, processes, and protocols without predicting for them what is to come. We can make things harder than they actually need to be.

Consistency is particularly important during times of change. Jeffrey M. Hiatt, in his book *ADKAR,* talks about this. *ADKAR* is an acronym for Awareness, Desire, Knowledge, Ability, and Reinforcement. Under the topic of growing awareness, he discusses the creditability of the sender. He mentions that the level of trust and respect of the person initiating the change will determine how the change is accepted and processed. We can build others' trust and respect in us when we show up consistently. And because of that, we can lead them in change. Once again, it is apparent that leadership is more about how we show up than what we know. It is simply not enough to just know the leadership strategies; we must know how to show up and be there for people. That's what separates the good from the great leaders.

Step into consistent contentment

Build consistency in how you show up for others and for yourself as well. Be consistent in your walk with God, in your relationships with others, and in your self-care. We can't be there for others if we aren't there for ourselves. What does this mean?

Start with developing a spirit of contentment which emerges from gratitude. We aren't grateful because we are content; we are content because we are grateful. Cultivate your personal gratitude and be intentional about your efforts. When we are content, we can steer away from complaining.

Let's look at the Old Testament for an example. Moses, a leader we could all learn from, was trying to lead the people through the desert. They began with grumbling in Exodus 16:1-3. You would think they would be trusting because they saw God's direction. Instead, Moses pointed out that their grumbling was a complaint against God. Sometimes those you are leading may get caught up in complaining. Your job is to help them see the purpose and direction you are wanting them to go.

This process is all dependent on trust. It seems that we either come from a place of trust or from a perspective of complaining. I am wondering how Moses felt when all those he was trying to lead spent most of their time grumbling and complaining. It was probably pretty evident that they didn't trust him. And more importantly, they didn't trust God's provision. You may encounter this when you are leading because those you are leading may not trust you as you lead them into uncharted waters. Build your trust by being trustworthy. Consistency and calm contribute to trustworthiness. And once again, we circle back to the premise that leadership is about how you show up rather than what you know.

Contentment is created from consistent gratitude. This is something I do for spurts and then get complacent and find myself in a place of grumbling. It takes me a while to realize my detour, and then I try to re-route and re-commit to my personal gratitude practice. Sometimes insight only comes after I find myself in a place I don't want to be—that of negativity. And then I do my best to shift and go back to a focus on all the things I am grateful for. Do whatever works for you. Make a list, journal your gratitude, meditate on those things that are pure, pray and give God thanks. This is the foundation for a life full of contentment, a life where you honor God by how you show up as a leader who isn't always striving for more.

I don't know about you, but I don't want to live a life where I am constantly comparing myself to others to determine my worth. It is unfair to compare because you will always find someone in a better position than you, more talented than you, smarter than you, and even more successful than you. If that is your focus, you won't be able to realize and appreciate where you are and who you are. To manage this, stay away from social media where people are centered on image and impressing. That can encourage you to feel not good enough. It's better to just limit your exposure.

Step into growth spurts

Sometimes we go through growth spurts. Sometimes we get feedback, sometimes we mess things up, and sometimes we learn something new. Several times in my career, I got the message that someone wanted to give me feedback—words you don't really want to hear. My first inclination was to go bury my head and never emerge. Well, after prayer, maybe a trip to Starbucks, and some quiet reflection, I was ready to show up for courageous conversations. Listening to feedback is never easy, yet this is how we learn and grow. I would prefer being able to read a book and right my course, however it doesn't seem that is a realistic option. At least that is not how it usually happens for me.

What I've learned is that I need to be prayed up before I enter the spaces of difficult conversations. God gives us the peace that passes all understanding so we can show up in humility and as teachable. One of the things I didn't know that I needed to learn was to just own where I miss the mark. Oh, I really don't like allowing my flaws to be apparent to my colleagues, and yet, they see them. I am learning to acknowledge that I blew it, to validate the concerns raised and apologize or take accountability for what I'm hearing. In this pause, I feel that my growth increases exponentially. Others can see my taking responsibility and an unintended consequence is that I feel good about myself in the process.

By responding this way, I am living according to my values. I am showing up as teachable, humble, and honoring God in the journey. I wish I could say that it's easy for me, but it's not. The reality is that I am committed to this process even though it's difficult. Don't quit too soon. Growth spurts may make you want to give it up, and yet your best self may be right around the corner. If you fall, get back up and look for those who will give you a hand. Find those that won't shame you, they will show up with love and encouragement while acknowledging your struggles. My friends, that person is special and someone to hold onto.

To grow, we need to stay current. Being current involves currency in relationships—not holding grudges or a lack of forgiveness as well as being up to date in your professional field. When we stay current, we are living and working from a place of purpose and peace.

Steps to Growing

1. Invest in yourself and your professional growth. Realize that you are worthy of the investment.
2. Evaluate what is important to you and seek that in your

job opportunities. Try to not compromise your values because a title, salary or position looks appealing. Stay centered in your values and what is important to you.

3. Use your voice to get what you need and want. Don't be afraid to ask.

4. Find ways to create authenticity in your personal and professional lives. And connect with those who share your same values.

5. Embrace courage over comfort. Manage your fear so that you don't let it shut you down. Ask God to fill you with His courage.

6. Develop your consistency as a leader. Figure out what motivates you, address the things that will derail you, and build your self-awareness.

7. Create contentment through building trust in God's plan for your life. Engage in gratitude practices to build your contentment muscle.

8. Take breaks when things become intense and be sure to recharge in the process. Remember that you are the tool, so you need to keep the tool sharp and ready. Fill your bucket so that you can help to fill the buckets of others.

9. Step into growth spurts because that is where we learn the most. Don't be afraid of the discomfort that comes from being stretched or from growing. The hard part usually occurs right before things get better. Don't abandon the journey when it gets hard. Push through.

Success may be just over the hump or on the other side of your pain or discomfort.

10. Don't give up—find those that will talk you off the ledge. Those are your people. Cultivate those relationships as gold.

CHAPTER 8

Now you become the teacher

Step into being the teacher

Give it all away—your experiences, knowledge, wisdom, gifts, and learnings. Don't waste your journey. This is the time to celebrate all your experiences as you use them to pour into others. Be willing to share your flaws as well as your gifts. This creates the element of authenticity and allows others to show up in their less-than-perfect ways. Be gentle and kind as you share with others as you tune into their pace so they don't feel stress from their interactions with your leadership wisdom. We want them to be able to control the flow, not feel as though they are drinking from the fire hydrant. They may need to take sips instead.

Remember to ask others if they are okay with sharing your insights with them. You might state that you observed behaviors and responses, and you want to know if they would like to hear your insights, thoughts, and observations. By asking their opinion, you are giving them voice and choice to determine how they want to respond. If they aren't interested in your feedback, then move on. Don't camp out trying to convince them that they need your input. It could just be an issue of timing—this may not be the moment they are ready for feedback or growth.

Step into changing

Typically change doesn't occur by focusing on behaviors. My experience is that when we shift our language, we move our mindsets, which leads to changed behaviors. Think of it this way. One of your team members seems defiant and we label them as uncooperative. What if we created an alternative explanation for their behavior? What if we said they were struggling instead of uncooperative? Wouldn't your mindset shift from a place of judgment to a place of compassion? What if we changed the words we used to ones that demonstrate curiosity? Explore with good questions. What if you asked, "How might we…?" That type of question reduces defensiveness from the person being asked. Then you can engage in an authentic conversation. Isn't that what we all want and need? Even though it's difficult, we want to be seen and heard by someone we trust who won't shame or blame us. Those that speak into your life are so valuable. Be brave, be bold, speak into others with the Holy Spirit's leading. Be gentle with your words. When we engage in inquiry and exploration with others, our focus is relational. When we primarily seek information, our focus is on compliance and tasks. Remember this—invest your time in inquiry (asking good and clarifying questions) and exploration (How did this land with you? What are you thinking about?). As we explore, we may find new ways to connect and create.

Remind yourself to not take yourself too seriously. Sometimes we can be so intense and so hard on ourselves. I can really beat myself up when I mess up. I can easily spiral into shame. Then when I am caught up in that shame spiral, about the only thing that will pull me out is to call a friend who will give me the empathy I need for the moment. And remember that growth can take time, and failure is part of that journey.

We can't lead others where we aren't willing to go. If you aren't willing to challenge yourself, how can you challenge others? As leaders, we get the privilege of setting the tone by our behaviors and words. And with that privilege comes the responsibility of managing ourselves as we lead others. This is simple yet not easy because so many variables come into play. Our personal lives affect how we lead. At times our personal stresses factor in and keep us from being able to regulate our emotions. I know the times that finances are an issue or when my husband and I are at odds, those are the times that I don't show up emotionally regulated. Being aware of my personal challenges can help me to not succumb to reactionary responses.

For example, not long after my dad died, I found myself lacking focus and on edge. Fortunately, I took a pause to determine what was going on with me. I wasn't very self-aware at that moment, so I needed time to reflect. Upon my reflection, I realized that I was in a grief moment. It took a pause for me to see that I was spiraling in my grief. Then came the work of giving myself compassion and grace while I moved through various emotional responses. I didn't need to stay stuck in my distress—it was enough to acknowledge it. Then I could tell my colleagues that I wasn't in a good space and needed an extra measure of grace.

Don't we all need moments of extra grace poured on us? I don't know about you, I need grace in buckets daily. And because God gives us grace, we can give it to others in abundance. You can't give what you don't have. And as we let grace pass through us, we absorb some of whatever flows through us. This is a double blessing. We give others what we receive ourselves. Who wouldn't want that? Sometimes we may find that it is much easier to give others grace while it is difficult to do the same for ourselves. We need to remember that we are worthy of grace as much as those we love and care for. Ask yourself, as well as those you supervise, what do I want and what do I need?

Step into being present

While on this journey, stay in the present. Try to avoid being historical as bringing up the past may not be helpful. Let go of what you can't control, or you may end up frustrated and angry. Additionally, step into your feelings and don't try to avoid or diminish them. Own them and move through them. If you feel sad, feel all the sadness so you can move on. It is when we short-circuit our process that those feelings will continue to show up. If we process through them and discharge them, we can move to healing and that is when we are most open to God's plans in our life. Stay in your emotions until you are ready to move on. There isn't a rush. Somewhere we began to believe that it's not okay to not be okay. Remember that we all experience moments when we're not okay; that is part of humanity.

When you are in the change process, be sure to attend to the emotional and relational components. Tend to the people and let them know you care. Be mindful and present. Express your own emotions during the journey. Be real. Be aware of the difficulties that change brings to most people. While we may be capable of stretching, achieving, and changing, we may find ourselves trapped by our self-imposed walls of doubt, fear, anxiety, or other emotional stressors. Our role as leaders may be to help others see over their barriers. We need to start with seeing over own walls first.

One helpful exercise is to visualize three buckets:
1. Let it go
2. Fix it
3. Don't let it go; don't fix it

There are some things you just need to let go; you can't control or fix them. The only progress will happen when they are released. Some things need to be fixed—you need to invest the time and energy to make them better. Often I feel that I need to fix everything when the reality is that I only need to fix certain things. The bucket of don't let it go and don't fix it may be where you put those things that you aren't ready to do anything with or you are conflicted about them; however, you need to be careful to not just dump all of your unpleasant things there. You can make intentional choices about where specific tasks or decisions need to be placed. You can use this tool to determine how to respond when situations overwhelm you. Just being able to name your stressors helps you to tame them.

Step into being your best self

Titus 3:1 tells us to be ready to do whatever is good. Build your character by doing what is good in private rather than focusing on your image, which is what you put out in public. Our public image is just that—an image that we can construct. Your character is about who you are in whatever setting you are in. I know multiple leaders who are primarily focused on how others see them rather than how God sees them. It seems that social media promotes images rather than highlighting your character. Your influence is based on your input—who is giving you yours? Is God's input your priority? Do you spend time grounding yourself in God's word, with His people, and in listening to His direction for you? I find that I show up in ways that aren't my best self when I am leaning on my own talents, strengths or ideas. When I rely only on myself, my cup runs dry. When I fill my cup with God's plan for me; that's when I find that He equips me in mighty ways. It's important that I allocate the time and energy to seek God.

Here are 5 ways you can become an influencer:

1. Stay present; limit your distractions so you can be focused and give others your full attention. They deserve nothing less.

2. Attend to your character, not just your image. Ground yourself in God's word, His people, and His input.

3. Be intentional about who you want to be so you can live from your values. Ask God to refine you and be open to His correction. Ask others for feedback as Proverbs 27:17 tells us that iron sharpens iron.

4. Teach others in a gentle manner. Be kind and grace-filled.

5. Be generous—with your time, energy, knowledge, and feedback.

Identify ways you can build your influence:

_____

_____

_____

_____

Step into intention

Another challenge for me is when I show up with positive intent and then end up with an impact that I didn't want or plan for. It is difficult when things don't go the way that I thought they would. I may intend to be encouraging to someone, and they see my words as patronizing or critical. No matter what my intent is I am still responsible to see where my words or actions landed. This is where you need to invite feedback. My good intentions are not enough; the impact is what I need to attend to.

This is where the use of Emotional Intelligence can be beneficial. There are five components that comprise Emotional Intelligence:

- Self-Awareness
- Self-Regulation
- Empathy
- Motivation
- Social Skills

Many scholars say that self-awareness is the most important element with empathy a close second. If you are self-aware and self-regulated, you can observe how your words or actions impact others. At that point, you can then clarify or redo your response to align more closely with your intended impact.

For example, sometimes I want to give feedback about someone's presentation style. While I am doing this to help another person grow, it can come across as critical. If I see it land harshly on someone, I pivot and gentle my approach. This is where I am living aligned with my values while also staying true to my commitment to help others develop. And I want to make sure that I am kind and generous in the process. It can be so very difficult to give others feedback, and we can't shy away from this just because the process is difficult. Use your emotional intelligence, insight, and wisdom from the Holy Spirit to make sure that your impact lines up with your intent. That is the sweet spot and may take practice to achieve.

While we only talked about our intentions, we need to look at others' intentions and know that we need to be generous in not assigning intentionality to another's behaviors. While someone may come across gruff or terse, you can take a moment to assume positive intent. Perhaps they are tired or stressed. Any number of variables may contribute to a less than positive response. We need to not jump to conclusions or make judgments based on what we see; rather, give grace to determine what might be really happening for others. By even entertaining an alternative explanation, we are leading with grace.

Truth without grace can be mean, and grace without truth can be meaningless. Truth with grace creates trust and healing.

Use your words on purpose, for purpose, and with purpose. Others will appreciate you for the effort.

Part of being your best self is to dream. Do not ask how, just dream. Think. Imagine. Jeremiah 30:2 tells us "This is what the Lord, the God of Israel says: 'Write in a book all the words I have spoken to you.'" And Habakkuk 2:2 says, "'Write down the revelation and make it plain on tablets…'" Perhaps you need to create a vision board, asking God to impart His plan for you. Write it down, draw it, or use pictures from magazines. Capture your dream as God speaks to us because this is often how He shows us His plan for our lives. Take a moment and date the vision He gives you so that you can mark that date and refer back to it.

Step into generosity

Work from a place of abundance, not scarcity. Be generous with your compassion, grace, and praise. Be generous with your energy and time. Be generous with your self-compassion as well. Listen more, speak less, and don't freak out. Be generous with paying attention to others. Are you noticing a theme here?

Create a legacy of generosity. Give and it shall be given to you. Give without holding back. Don't focus on being or having enough. Give with abandonment for that is when God blesses the most. And because God is our resource, He will grant us all we need. Trust the process.

Generosity creates joy. We often think that we will be generous out of our joy, yet much like most of God's precepts, the opposite is true. This is that bliss that we all crave and need. The joy sustains us. When our hearts fill with gladness, there isn't room for complaining and whining. God doesn't minimize the fact that we experience struggles, because when joy is our lens, we focus more on what He's done for us, which gives us perspective. Choose joy and set that as your intention. Generous people are happier.

Step into waiting

When things get challenging, we tend to go toward our go-to responses Sometimes we fight through, avoid people or situations, or we even freeze up. Those are our trauma responses—perhaps from our earlier work experiences or from childhood interactions. In contrast, God tells us to wait. Slow your roll. Waiting isn't passive. It is an active response because waiting means we are trusting in who God is and what His plan is for us.

When we wait, we are still. When we are still, we can hear God's voice. "Cease striving and know that I am God…" (Psalm 46:10). It is in this quiet place that we can hear and reflect. Tap into your calm. Others will gravitate toward you.. Isn't that worth the wait? This is the best position to hear God speak to you.

Moses knew to wait on God even when others were grumbling, complaining, and doubting God. He trusted who God is, His promises, and His presence. He told the Israelites to stop and remember all that God did for them; first with our salvation and then throughout our life when He provided for us in His perfect way with His perfect timing. And that, my friends, is worth the wait. Sometimes because of our roles we don't feel as though we can slow down, too many people depend on us and we must act. Be careful to not be caught up in that self-talk. Remember the important without getting caught up in what seems the most urgent for the moment.

Debi Grebenik, Ph.D.

Step into arriving

Let's pretend we arrived in our leadership journey. What did you learn on your trip? What will you carry with you? What did you miss or would do differently? What do you want to leave behind? Would you course-correct? Were there any surprises? Take a few moments to look at your leadership journey to this point. Ask God to show you His plan for your future while also taking time to reflect all He's brought you through to this point. Like how you would make a rest stop on a road trip, stop and make one now. Perhaps you need to refuel, get a snack, refresh, or even make new plans.

As you reflect, be sure to remember that leadership isn't about what you know or do, it's how you show up. So many teachings emphasize using a stiff upper lip and toughing it out. Let's change that narrative and focus on the healthy, emotional, physical, and spiritual benefits we gain by letting out the stressors. There's no such thing as failure—it's only feedback on how to move forward differently with lessons learned.

Lean into your emotional intelligence. Build your self-awareness; manage your emotional regulation and demonstrate empathy throughout your journey. Recently I engaged in a conversation where someone shared with me some things that needed attention. I wish I could say this was an easy conversation; however, the truth is that it was very difficult. I agonized about it, knowing it was coming yet not knowing what the content would be. Isn't it disconcerting when you know something challenging is ahead without knowing exactly what it will include? I spent a lot of time in prayer to prepare myself. And it even appeared the sermon that weekend was taught especially for me.

You know how the Holy Spirit works when He wants us to hear His message. I can honestly say that I spent a lot of time listening to the person giving me the feedback and experienced a calm that only God could create. I was able to tell the person thank you and that I appreciated their initiating a difficult conversation with me. I did my best to not be defensive or try to explain myself. And I meant it. I showed up more committed to courage than comfort. That doesn't mean that I like the process; I get my feelings hurt just like you do. I want to appear competent and be seen as successful. It's hard to sit in the uncomfortable spot of my flaws, my mistakes, and my weaknesses. And the Lord was whispering quietly to me that He was in control; that I needed to trust Him. And this truly became another opportunity to grow, to become more like Jesus.

I wish the growth just came, that we didn't need to go through the challenges to grow. I love the metaphor of the tulip where the bulb must push through the darkness of the dirt to emerge in all its beauty. The struggle through the darkness creates the beauty. I hope you are willing to move through the dirt toward the son. That is where the glory is. Don't expect it to be easy. Yet it is so worth it.

When I let go of that expectation, I can embrace difficult feedback because I know that's the only way to grow. I thought that at this stage of my career I could just coast. And that's not a realistic option. To just coast means that I am not growing, I am just maintaining, and that isn't an option. If we aren't growing, we are dying. Growth takes investment, energy, and commitment. I am all in. I want to keep growing and becoming a better version of myself—who God created me to be.

What are your intentions for your growth trajectory? How can you develop your knowledge, your insights, your skills, and your presence? Will you put energy toward how you show up, not just your knowledge? Who do you want to be in six months, one year, five years, or maybe ten years?

Live the pause

One definition of pause is to stop temporarily or to linger for a time. https://www.merriam-webster.com/dictionary/pause. Our lives tend to be so full that we don't pause or create any space. It is in that space or pause that we can hear the Holy Spirit. During that pause we can gather information, perhaps talk to others, pray about it and not act.

Another element of a pause is that you can take time to notice. Noticing is observing or paying attention to something. Noticing is the art of becoming aware of. Once we pause and increase our awareness, we can make an informed decision. Once we make our decisions, we can submit them to the Holy Spirit to proof by affirming them. When there is only a spirit of confusion, that is not of God; the giver of peace. Psalm 46:10 tells us that God is not a God of confusion; He is a God of peace.

Our calendars are not built for moments of pause. We must build them in and prioritize them. The benefits are significant. My pauses take the form of a walk around the block between Zoom calls, reading a book during down times, calling a friend, or just stretching and taking time to think.

Now as you pause and ponder your leadership journey, capture your thoughts. Ask the Holy Spirit to make your pathway clear. Pray, pause, and ponder…He will speak to you in those moments.

Step into developing others

1. Step into being the teacher where you give it all away—your expertise, your experience, and your energy. Give lavishly and you will receive in abundance. This is how God works.
2. Be generous with intention. Lead from a place of abundance rather than scarcity. Scarcity says there isn't enough and there will never be enough.
3. Cultivate contentment. Generosity + contentment = joy. Set joy as your intention. Joy is a practice that we can cultivate.
4. Feel your feelings. Don't shut them down. Let them speak to you and learn from them. Make self-awareness a priority.
5. Take time for reflection and resetting your journey. Maybe you need to change your course. Be open to the Spirit's leading.
6. Be willing to wait. Don't rush the process. Show up with patience and look for insight on what to do next or where you need to go. Let the journey unfold. Wait on the Lord. This only happens when we are still and can hear or listen to what it is that the Lord wants to tell us.
7. Invite feedback. Listen and hear without defensiveness.
8. Choose courage over comfort. That is where the real growth occurs.
9. Study and build your emotional intelligence. It will serve you well in your leadership roles. Infuse the concepts into your work language and into your supervisory conversations.

10. Above all, show empathy with those you work with.

Pause and consider what your next steps will be. Rather than trying to do multiple things at once, focus on one thing. Where will you start? Write down where you will start; perhaps capture other things you want to do or that you need to pay attention to. These can be tangible actions, or attitudes, or attributes you desire to build.

Next steps:

_____

_____

_____

_____

Scriptures that God is using to proof my plan:

_____

_____

_____

_____

References

All Scripture is New International Version unless otherwise noted.

Citations

Brown, B. (2013). *Daring greatly: How the courage to be vulnerable transforms the way we live, love, parent and lead.* New York: Avery Publishing Group.

DePree, M. (1989). *Leadership is an art.* New York: Knopf Publishing Group.

Heifetz, R.A., Linsky, M. (2017). *Leadership on the line: staying alive through the dangers of change.* New York: Harvard Business Review Publishing.

Sinek, S. (2009). *Start with why: how great leaders inspire everyone to take action.* New York: Portfolio.

About the Author

Debi Grebenik trains internationally and is known for her expertise in healing trauma, leading change, and teaching others in their professional development.

Her education includes Masters' Degrees in Social Work and Religious Education; and a Ph.D. from the University of Colorado. Additionally, as a pastor's wife for 43 years, she loves people and the church.

She founded the Trauma Training Institute which focuses on training and coaching on trauma competent interventions and strategies. She also co-authored "Crossing the Deep Waters of Trauma, Trials, and Loss." This Bible study is a favorite among those healing from trauma, grief or loss because of its non-traditional approach and authentic conversations.

Debi's mission is for everyone to have an "aha" moment about the impact of trauma on their personal and professional lives. What she is best known for is her love of the color pink, her 8 grandchildren and Starbucks as well as her nonstop energy.

•dgrebenik@gmail.com •719.360.6335 • @dgrebenik
•Facebook: Trauma Training Institute and
Crossing the Deep Waters

www.ingramcontent.com/pod-product-compliance
Lightning Source LLC
Chambersburg PA
CBHW071356160426
42811CB00112B/2307/J